Teatime

—*to*—

Tailgates

Teatime
— to —
Tailgates

---

150 YEARS AT THE K-STATE TABLE

---

*Hope you enjoy these stories about
a great place and great folks.*

By Jane P. Marshall

College of Human Ecology

Kansas State University

THE
DONNING COMPANY
PUBLISHERS

Virginia Moxley, dean of the College of Human Ecology from 2006 to 2013, was the yeast for this project, the college's gift to Kansas State University as it celebrates its sesquicentennial.

The Virginia Munson Moxley Excellence Fund provided seed money for the project. Proceeds from the sales of Teatime to Tailgates *will return to the fund supporting research and international study opportunities for undergraduate students in Human Ecology.*

FRONT ENDSHEET: Professor Nellie Kedzie has tea with Ruth Stokes, a student, in her office in Anderson Hall, ca. 1885. COURTESY OF MORSE DEPARTMENT OF SPECIAL COLLECTIONS, KANSAS STATE UNIVERSITY LIBRARIES

BACK ENDSHEET: Fans flock to tailgate parties at every home football game, dining on burgers to gourmet cuisine and wearing purple, 2010. COURTESY OF DAVID MAYES, KANSAS STATE UNIVERSITY DIVISION OF COMMUNICATIONS AND MARKETING

COVER PHOTOS:
TOP: Cherry pie is a Kansas icon. Linda P. Thurston baked the pie on the cover. PHOTOGRAPH BY JANE P. MARSHALL

BOTTOM, LEFT TO RIGHT:
Willie the Wildcat isn't the only one wild about K-State ice cream. COURTESY OF DAVID MAYES, KANSAS STATE UNIVERSITY DIVISION OF COMMUNICATIONS AND MARKETING

Graduate students learn about sensory research in food and beverages in the Sensory Analysis Center lab. COURTESY OF MATT BINTER, KANSAS STATE UNIVERSITY DIVISION OF COMMUNICATIONS AND MARKETING

Even in the early K-State classroom, pie was on the Kansas menu, undated. COURTESY OF MORSE DEPARTMENT OF SPECIAL COLLECTIONS, KANSAS STATE UNIVERSITY LIBRARIES

Today's home kitchens seldom produce old-fashioned favorites such as tomato preserves and watermelon pickles. PHOTOGRAPH BY JANE P. MARSHALL

TITLE PAGE: PHOTOGRAPH BY DAVID MAYES, KANSAS STATE UNIVERSITY DIVISION OF COMMUNICATIONS AND MARKETING

The Donning Company Publishers
184 Business Park Drive, Suite 206
Virginia Beach, VA 23462

Anne Burns, *Editor*   Kathy Adams, *Imaging Artist*
Stephanie Danko, *Graphic Designer*   Barry Haire, *Project Director*

Library of Congress Cataloging-in-Publication Data

Marshall, Jane, 1945-
        Teatime to tailgates : 150 years at the K-State table / by Jane P. Marshall, College of Human Ecology, Kansas State University.
            pages cm
        Includes bibliographical references and index.
        ISBN 978-1-57864-858-0
1. Cooking, American—Midwestern style. 2. Cooking—Kansas. 3. Kansas State University—History. I. Title.
        TX715.2.M53M37 2013
        641.59781—dc23
                                                                        2013029120

Printed in the United States of America at Walsworth Publishing Company

Contents

Foreword

RECIPES ARE LIKE THE MOON, revealing time, season, geography.

They reflect the kitchen equipment, ingredients and taste trends of the day.

They reflect the progress of science, the preoccupations of the family cook, the state of the nation and the world.

Recipes reflect the culinary skills of the cook. Recipes in early America needed few instructions; women knew how to cook. Today, the best cookbooks give detailed directions, explaining now only how but why, to inexperienced but eager cooks.

The recipes in this book tell the same stories. I have tried to keep those stories as accurate as possible. A few of the recipes have been adjusted to fit modern ingredients and modern equipment. In many cases, instructions have been edited for consistency and clarity.

Most are still true to the era in which they were written. However, I have added "or butter" to most that call for margarine. Butter has swung back into favor. The glamour of margarine and of cooking with shortening has waned.

Some recipes are untouched. One is Orange Kiss-Me Cake, printed exactly as I received it because the directions are filled with the cook's personality. Another is Nellie Kedzie's Prune Soufle which is indicative of the era. Nearly all the recipes—well, not the roast raccoon—have been tested in a modern kitchen.

Acknowledgments

THANKS TO:

My Grandmother Flora Coverdill Pretzer, my mother Marianne Simmons Pretzer and my twin sister Linda Pretzer Thurston who remind me that cooking, heart and soul are forever linked. My friend Janet Johnson and my friend Terry Thompson Anderson who remind me that kitchen time is adventure time. My husband Thom Marshall who washes the pots and pans just for me. My daughters Clara Garrett Marshall Sackrider and Hannah Mary Marshall who make me whole. My graduate history professors at the University of St. Thomas in Houston who allowed me to do all my research on food. To all the editors and reporters over the years who nourished my passion for writing facts and telling stories. And to my cheerleading squad—Martha Buess, Jennifer Rettele-Thomas, Debby Hiett, Deb Canter, Sally Yahnke—for the encouraging words. To Cheryl Collins and Linda Glasgow at the Riley County Historical Society for letting me pick their brains and paw through their archives. To K-State colleagues Dave Mayes, Marla Day, Cliff Hight, Tony Crawford, Pat Patton, Mary Molt, Michelle Netson and others mentioned throughout the book for exceptional assistance and essential exceptionalness.

And thanks to those on whose shoulders we stand, those men and women who built community, raised families, established businesses, were the caretakers of the intellectual and the physical environments and still took time to grasp the world by the horns and make a difference in how people eat and what they eat. They mentor us, challenge us. We remember them, thank them, we promise to continue.

Most importantly, thanks to the farmers, hugs and kisses to the cooks. And vice versa.

Introduction

THE STORY OF FOOD on the Kansas State University table is the story of food in Kansas.

It is the story of grasshoppers and drought, of tornadoes and blizzards. It is the story of fortitude and patience, of the love of independence and the bravery of risk. It is the story of men and women who loved the horizon, the land and a good loaf of bread.

Have we changed? Of course. Our tans are now sought instead of earned. We seldom buck bales of hay or shovel wheat or milk cows or chase chickens for dinner; we exercise in gyms wearing expensive shoes. We spend too much time on computers and in front of television sets. We spend too little time in awe of Kansas sunsets and watching baby bluebirds fledge.

But Kansans are still fiercely loyal to their roots, sunk deep in the fertile loam. We still hold independence dear. We are still strong of spirit and inclined toward adventure.

If asked, would we leave family behind and head west as those early Kansans did? I think so, although we might try to stick the iPad and KitchenAid in a corner of the covered wagon.

If asked, would we walk to a neighbor's to help with a barn raising

The 19th century trail drive "cookie" served as banker, doctor, dentist, barber, baker, cook, peacekeeper and ruler of the chuck wagon for around $45 a month. PHOTOGRAPH BY JANE P. MARSHALL

or a child birthing? I think so, if we could fit it into our absurdly packed iCal.

We still value hard work. We still care about our neighbors. We still put up a good fight for what we believe in.

For 150 years K-State graduates have used their

Fried chicken dinner Kansas style. PHOTOGRAPH BY JANE P. MARSHALL

education to feed and nurture families and communities, to build economies and cities and better mousetraps, to educate the next generations for the challenges ahead.

Generations of students left K-State with shiny purple degrees. Some stayed in Kansas. Others settled in Australia or Estonia or Dallas. Wherever they landed, they kept memories of the food they ate and the friends they made during their years in Wildcat land. Sometimes what we remember and cherish is "not the food itself but all the bonds and memories the food represents," says Chef Michael Chiarello.

This book reflects that. Many shared their recipes and stories. More information about food on the K-State table came from archives, diaries, newspapers and other references.

K-State helps set the table of the world with its research and with the hearty influence of its faculty and graduates who are dietitians, chefs, writers, restaurateurs, Extension agents, teachers and more.

Together they form a picture of the rich food heritage of the nation's first land-grant institution.

The purpose of this book is to celebrate that 150-year-old heritage. I want you to say, "Ah yes. I remember that. Meet you in the kitchen." I want you to have a Purple Pot Luck and sing "Happy Birthday" to K-State. I want you to appreciate K-State's legacy that continues from teatime to tailgates and beyond.

Most of all, I want you to heed that old saying—"thank the farmer and kiss the cook." In Kansas, and much of the rest of the world, when you do that you also thank Kansas State University.

·|·

Teatime

on

Frontier's Edge

A BRAND NEW KANSAS STATE AGRICULTURAL COLLEGE perched on a pastoral hill in the middle of chaos and wilderness. The year was 1863 and in every direction the New England professors and their young Kansas students were surrounded by bloodshed and bravery, hope and heartbreak.

A few miles north of Manhattan, pioneers traveled west on the Oregon Trail in search of an agricultural paradise, gold wealth and adventure.

To the south, frontiersmen and women, traders and military traversed the Santa Fe Trail, a major trade route between the mercantile hub in Missouri and the New Mexico Territory city of Santa Fe. They stopped in Council Grove, Kansas, to restock food supplies.

To the southeast, the Civil War raged. William Quantrill burned and killed nearly 200 in Lawrence that year. The bloodletting didn't reach as far as Manhattan and the little college on the hill west of town—although abolitionist and pro-slavery sentiments certainly did. Citizens felt its pinch and, in the struggle between the North and the South, they grieved, made room for worn Union soldiers and held strong their convictions as they welcomed displaced former slaves and sheltered runaways.

John Breukelman described in *Kansas Natural History in 1863*: "Except for the Santa Fe Trail and a few military trails and forts, the western half of Kansas looked much as it had for thousands of years."

Fort Riley was built in 1853 to guard the Santa Fe and Oregon trails and maintain order when the territory opened to settlers in 1854. Indians still crisscrossed the land, hunting, raiding and trying unsuccessfully to hold onto their way of life. The last Indian battle in Kansas, with the Cheyenne, was in 1878. By 1885, the bison, which once roamed the territory in herds of hundreds of thousands, had all but vanished in Kansas.

Emigrants on Train, Boat, Wagon and Foot

These westering men and women spent a minimum of $500 (19th century money) to outfit their trip to a new life. Add a wagon and draft animals, the bill could easily become $1,000.

Many bought supplies at Westport or St. Joseph, Missouri. They were advised to take enough provisions for the trip, which took 3 to 6 months depending on their destination. Their shopping list, per person, could look like this:

- ⚜ 200 pounds flour or crackers
- ⚜ 150 pounds bacon
- ⚜ 10 pounds coffee

- ❖ 20 pounds sugar
- ❖ 10 pounds salt
- ❖ chipped beef, rice, tea, beans, dried fruit, vinegar, and tallow to make soap and candles

Gear included a coffee pot, tin plates, cups, knives, forks, a kettle and frying pan. Some included a keg of pickles or kraut. Provisions took up most of the room in a wagon.

One traveler wrote, "I suggest to each family the propriety of taking a small sheet-iron cooking stove with fixtures, as the wind and rain often times renders it almost impossible to cook without them."

Weight was a major consideration. Diarists told of exhausted animals unable to pull heavy wagons up mountains or ravines. Women made minute adjustments so they might carry a precious sewing machine or cook stove or organ. Many carried dried baked bread, lighter and less prone to mold.

In the midst of the dust and disorder, women tried to make their wagons livable.

"Through all the winter preceding the April morning when the final start was made, the fingers of the women and girls were busy providing additional stores of bedding and blankets," recalled one diarist. Despite the warnings to leave large or heavy items at home, "the emigrants filled wagon fitted up in the best possible style, carpeted, with chairs, bed and looking glass for the convenience of families," was one report.

Food was monotonous and often muddy and raw or gritty with trail dust.

Similar conditions plagued cowboys and drovers who used to plead: "Spit in my ears and tell me lies, but give me no more dried apple pies." They never complained to Cookie's face, however. A cowboy did not want to make an enemy of the camp cook. Another cowboy saying was "Only a fool argues with a skunk, a mule or a cook."

Dried apples, often dirty and leather-like, were a mainstay on the frontier. One pioneer recipe simply calls for washing the dried apples thoroughly, soaking them overnight in water. In the morning, stew slowly in the soaking water until tender. Sweeten to taste. "The crust, both upper and under, should be rolled thin; a thick crust to a fruit pie is undesirable."

Settlers in Manhattan missed fresh fruit that grew in their home states. They planted fruit trees at the same time they built houses and started businesses, then changed their culinary skills to match their new environment.

By 1871 the college had planted 2,100 apple, pear, peach, cherry and plum trees in the college orchard. Students were helping grow more in the nursery.

The need for dried apples faded as apple trees grew in prairie orchards and railroads hauled apples to the plains. Cooks stored the fall apple crops in "cyclone" cellars.

If you hanker to revisit dessert on the trail or on the homestead, try baking a pie in cast iron over coals. (Skip the authenticity of a buffalo chip fire.) These instructions on baking a pie in a cast iron pan come from Barbara Swell whose son, Wes Erbsen, is doing graduate work in physics at K-State. She teaches cooking classes at the John C. Campbell Folk School in Brasstown, North Carolina, and at her Log Cabin Cooking School in Asheville, North Carolina.

By 1880, 2,386,812 apple trees had been planted in Kansas for commercial and home use. The K-State campus grew an extensive orchard, 2013. COURTESY OF DAVID MAYES, KANSAS STATE UNIVERSITY DIVISION OF COMMUNICATIONS AND MARKETING

How To Bake a Pie in a Cast Iron Pan

From Barbara Swell

You can bake any pie in a cast iron pan, but it's easiest to start with fruit pies that have a solid or lattice-top crust. Have the pie filled, chilled and ready to go. You can bake with either campfire or fireplace embers, or, if you want a more predictable experience, try packaged charcoal briquettes. About 15 hot briquette coals on top and 11 underneath should give you a 375-degree oven. Have plenty of extra briquettes or embers handy, as I find I always need to replenish halfway through the bake.

To bake the equivalent of a 9-inch pie in a shallow glass pie plate, you'll need a 12-inch cast iron Dutch oven with feet and recessed top. Lodge makes them and they're widely available for camping or hearth cooking. You'll also need 3 canning jar lids. Put the canning jar lids in the bottom of your iron pot and replace the lid. To pre-heat your oven, place a shovelful of embers under the empty pot and another on top of the lid. Wait about 15 minutes and remove the lid (a lid-lifter is a handy tool, and they're sold where you purchase the Dutch ovens). Place your pie onto the canning jar rings and replace the lid. Refresh the coals if needed and check the pie after about 20 minutes. If it's getting brown too fast, then don't add any more coals. If nothing's happening, brush off the ashes and add a few more coals.

Bake the pie for 30 to 45 minutes, until the innards bubble and it's nicely browned. A little char here and there adds to the adventure! You'll need a hot pad and spatula to lift the pie out of the hot pot.

Rob Wall of Manhattan is cast iron crazy, hooked on the art of campfire cooking when his son was in Boy Scouts. He has shared his skills with students at University for Mankind, at Outdoor Woman gatherings, and Scouts. He adapted this recipe from a chuckwagon cookbook.

✧✧ COWBOY CABBAGE

From Rob Wall

½–1 pound bacon, chopped
1 onion, chopped
1 green pepper, chopped
1 teaspoon garlic powder
Salt to taste

Ground black pepper (lots of it)
Cajun seasoning
1 head cabbage, chopped
   (or 1–2 bags shredded cabbage)

Cook bacon until crisp in cast iron Dutch oven. Add onion and green pepper and cook until onion is translucent. Add garlic powder, salt, black pepper and Cajun seasoning. Stir in chopped cabbage. Cook until cabbage begins to limp.

Taste. Stir in more seasoning as needed. Serve warm.

Yield: 6 servings

Kansas or Bust: Some Stayed to Settle the Territory

The first census of 1854–55 recorded 3,000 settlers in the Kansas Territory. Like the Indians who lived here before them, the Kansas settlers planted corn, pumpkins and squash. They also planted fruit trees. "I think this demonstrated faith in 'what he sows so shall he reap,'" wrote one young Kansas diarist in the late 19th century.

Also like the Indians before them, they feasted and played games to celebrate good harvests and successful hunts in good times. They went hungry and watched helplessly as babies died during bad times.

Some built homes from patches of sod 2 feet long and 2 inches thick, layered in walls 2 to 3 feet thick. They hung Indian blankets (buffalo robes) across doorways. Others set up tents, home until limestone could be quarried or lumber hauled from the nearest mill.

The Homestead Act of 1862 provided 160 acres of land from the public domain to heads of households willing to live on the land and improve it by building a 12 by 14-foot dwelling and growing crops. The idea was that on 160 acres, a farmer could feed the family and sell surplus crops and livestock, thus turning farmers into businessmen.

More than 2 million applicants tried their hand at homesteading. An estimated 100,000 homesteaders gave up, some leaving signs that read, "In God we trusted, in Kansas we busted."

To all those who journeyed west, food meant sustenance and society. But for those settlers who stayed, food took a third meaning. Livelihood.

It is that core that fed the little college on the hill. Its leaders, students and coursework—although filled with shenanigans that would make even today's academic shudder—put together a formula for food that endures today. Food is sustenance. It is society. It is livelihood. At K-State all three areas are the work of scholarship and of contributions to the world.

Early settlers lived off the land and they planted seeds that would yield food quickly. They grew popcorn to use at home and to sell.

Early domestic science students learned practical skills, such as regulating oven temperature and baking bread, suited to living on the frontier, undated. COURTESY OF MORSE DEPARTMENT OF SPECIAL COLLECTIONS, KANSAS STATE UNIVERSITY LIBRARIES

❖❖ POPCORN PUDDING

From Nebraska Pioneer Cookbook

"Soak two quarts of freshly popped corn in three pints of sweet milk overnight. When ready to bake, add three well-beaten eggs, a little salt and sugar to taste. Bake like a custard pudding."

❖❖ MULLBERRY PIE

From Farm Journal's Country Cookbook

There are two ways to pick mulberries for a pie, according to this cookbook compiled by Nell Nichols, a 1916 graduate of K-State.

"The recipe for mulberry pie properly starts: Select a sunny summer day when the breezes are light. Stand on the shady side of the mulberry tree and fill your pail with the knobby, long, glistening berries.

"Or if you are of a different berry-picking school: Spread a worn sheet on the emerald grass beneath the tree, shake the branches lightly and run from the shower of juicy, warm, sweet berries that plop down."

This recipe combines the sweetness of mulberries with the tartness of rhubarb, which the pioneers called pie plant.

Pastry for 2-crust pie (page 79)   **¼ cup flour**
2 cups mulberries   **2 tablespoons butter**
1 cup finely sliced rhubarb   **or margarine**
1 cup sugar

Preheat oven to 425°F.

Combine mulberries and rhubarb in medium bowl. Combine sugar and flour. Sprinkle about half of the sugar mixture in bottom of pastry-lined 9-inch pie pan. Turn mulberries and rhubarb into pie pan and add remaining sugar-flour mixture. Dot with butter. Adjust top crust, cut steam vents and flute edges.

Bake 40 to 50 minutes, or until crust is browned and juices bubble in vents.

YIELD: 1 PIE

In a 2009 story in the *Kansas City Star*, Lee Hill Kavanaugh wrote about a Missouri trapper who sold raccoon meat for $3 to $7 an animal. He did a pretty good business. Raccoons, plentiful in eastern Kansas, sometimes ended up on the dinner table. Other wild animals did too. More than one family caught a possum, caged it and fed it milk, bread and a roasted potato or two for a few days "to clean it out."

ROAST RACCOON ✤ ✤

From Farm Journal's Country Cookbook *(1959)*

3 to 4 raccoons, 4 to 6 pounds each	2 cups flour
5 tablespoons salt	1 cup shortening
2 teaspoons pepper	8 medium onions, peeled
	12 small bay leaves

Skin, draw and clean raccoons soon after killing. Remove, without breaking, the brown bean-shaped kernels from under forelegs and each thigh.

Cut into pieces. Reserve meaty back and legs for baking. Cook bony pieces in water to make broth for gravy and stuffing. Add small amount of seasonings. Simmer until meat is tender; strain and use only the broth.

Sprinkle back and leg pieces with salt and pepper. Then dredge with flour. Heat shortening in heavy skillet. Add meat; brown on all sides. Transfer pieces to roaster; add onions and bay leaves. Cover.

Bake in 350°F oven for 2 hours or until tender. Make gravy by adding flour to drippings in pan. Use 2 to 3 tablespoons of flour for each cup of liquid or broth.

YIELD: 24 SERVINGS (AT LEAST)

Pemmican was adapted from the Indians who made the "fast food" from dried meat (often bison), meat fat and dried berries.

❖❖ PEMMICAN

From Nebraska Pioneer Cookbook

"Combine equal parts of buffalo suet; dried fruit such as cherries, berries and plums; and dried venison or game. Add salt if available, and pound the mixture in a bowl or a hollow rock; then form into bricks. Dry in the sun, or near the fire in rainy weather. Pemmican may be eaten as is, by biting off chunks, or bricks may be simmered in water to make a thick soup or stew."

Wooden wagons brought settlers and supplies to Kansas. PHOTOGRAPH BY JANE P. MARSHALL

Early settlers mixed scrapple from the scraps and trimmings of meat left over from hog butchering. They boiled the mixture in a big pot outdoors, molded it into a loaf and fried slices. The Pennsylvania Dutch (German) version used pork and cornmeal. Regional recipes vary wildly.

When the staff at Derby Dining Center changed the name of Scrapple to Breakfast Polenta, students gobbled it up. John Pence, associate director of housing and dining services, contributed this dining service recipe to a little book called *The Land of Ah's* published in 1982 by the Kansas Home Economics Association. It was called Scrapple then.

BREAKFAST POLENTA ✤ ✤
(formerly known as Scrapple)

From John Pence

1 cup cornmeal	1 pound whole hog sausage,
1 cup cold water	browned and drained
1 teaspoon salt	3 cups boiling water

Combine cornmeal, cold water and salt in large saucepan. Stir in sausage. Stir in boiling water, stirring constantly. Place over low heat, stirring occasionally. Pour into loaf pan and chill thoroughly.

To serve, turn out from loaf pan, slice thin and fry until crispy brown. Usually no additional fat is needed, but add a small amount of oil to skillet if sausage is extra lean. Serve piping hot with jelly or syrup.

Slice only as much as you need, wrap remainder in plastic wrap and store in refrigerator.

YIELD: 6 TO 8 SERVINGS

Manhattan: Building Schools, Starting Businesses

When Isaac Goodnow and the other Free-State immigrants moved to the Kansas Territory in 1855, the fare was simple. It was frontier food. They ate what they grew in their gardens, what they could trade or buy from neighbors, what was available at local shops.

Except for new-fangled items like Mr. Borden's condensed milk, canned oysters and the new leavening agent called saleratus (baking soda), most food came from within 50 miles of town. Non-local food was hauled to Manhattan by wagons or on river barges. Both modes of transportation were expensive and dangerous.

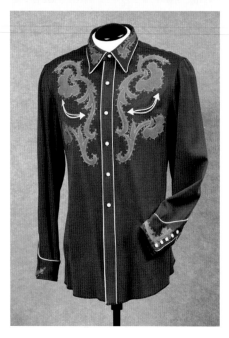

Western shirt, ca. 1950. Courtesy of David Mayes, Kansas State University Division of Communications and Marketing, K-State Historic Costume and Textile Museum, 2008.15.2. Gift of Bill and Laura Varney.

Goodnow and his fellow travelers in the New England Emigrant Aid Company had left comfortable lives in the east, drawn toward the Kansas Territory by the vision of opportunity and by the cause of abolition. Goodnow's group and the Cincinnati and Kansas Land Company united to form the city of Manhattan. The Cincinnati group was charged with the town's commerce, the New Englanders with "public education and morality."

Goodnow, a former natural science professor, believed in education on the frontier. He started planning a college immediately. In 1860 he, Samuel D. Houston, Joseph Denison, Washington Marlatt and several others opened Bluemont Central College, a primary and preparatory school associated with the Methodist Episcopal Church. After the passage of the federal Morrill Act establishing land-grant universities in 1862, the one-building college became Kansas State Agricultural College in 1863 and eventually Kansas State University.

The little town of Manhattan flourished on the intersection of the crystal clear Big Blue and the Kansas rivers. The Cincinnati group had brought a small gristmill, cooking stoves, seeds and agricultural implements with them on the *Hartford*, the 144-ton paddlewheel steamboat that brought them to Kansas Territory. Among the first businesses were August Winkler's mill on Fancy Creek and a flour mill in the downtown area.

Welsh, Swedish, Danish, Germans, Bohemians, Russians, Irish, Norwegians, Chez-Moravians, Swiss, English and more settled in the area. By 1863, Kansas had almost 200,000 people.

They survived landsharks and hooligans, grasshoppers and tornadoes, droughts and depressions.

Through all this, they tried to recreate the home and family culture they left behind. They tried to restore pre-migration food and dining rituals. From this effort grew K-State's food heritage, molded by the origins of its students, faculty and neighbors.

The food ethos dominating the American table for decades reflected the European religious traditions of the new Kansans. That is the belief that food is sustenance. One eats so one has the energy to work. One does not eat for the pleasure of it. That's gluttony and gluttony is a sin.

So the earliest K-State table—when that table was in private homes and boarding houses—would be set with meat and potatoes (or noodles) to nourish bodies that farmed, walked, herded and built. There was dessert. Not tables full of it of course, but enough to satisfy the Anglo-Saxon sweet tooth.

During the same era, food on the American table was undergoing an upheaval. Preservation, transportation, industrialization, technology and scientific discoveries touched those who grew, marketed, prepared and consumed dinner.

Kansas State University became a global player in that upheaval.

"A very nice apple something-or-other"

In the early days of K-State, domestic science classes (then called household economy) were in charge of college food, from student meals on campus to the Board of Regents meeting.

The university's second president, John A. Anderson, described a meal served to the Board of Regents in 1877, in the campus newspaper, *The Industrialist*:

The occasion excited all the more interest in the minds of both entertainers and guests because of the fact that this was not only the first effort of the class in this direction, but also

the first effort of the first class to whom the art of cooking has been taught in any college of the United States. The first course was delicately flavored soup, as good as any we ever tasted. It was followed by roast beef; Irish potatoes boiled; ditto fried; sweet potatoes boiled; jellied beef and cold roast pork. The dessert, which would charm both an epicure and a dyspeptic, consisted of Union pie, Washington pie, a very nice apple something-or-other, two or three kinds of cake, and coffee and apples.

John A. Anderson, president of K-State, 1873–1879. COURTESY OF MORSE DEPARTMENT OF SPECIAL COLLECTIONS, KANSAS STATE UNIVERSITY LIBRARIES

Washington Pie is similar to the modern-day Boston Cream Pie, which is really a cake: two layers of cake filled with a vanilla pudding, the top frosted with chocolate. *Fanny Farmer Cookbook* (11th edition) calls for two layers of butter or yellow cake, filled with raspberry jam and sprinkled with confectioner's sugar.

Another type of Washington Pie originated in Washington, D.C., before the Civil War. It was a square cake made of broken pieces of cake within a bottom and top pie crust. The cake pieces came from odds and ends of broken cakes that piled up in bakeries. Pieces were dampened with water and milk or cream. Bakers threw in raisins and spices and poured it onto a crust. It was baked in large pans, then cut and sold in squares. Some hotels and boarding houses covered the pie with sauce. These were also known as railroad cakes, according to a 1898 Washington newspaper article.

Another 1910 Washington Pie recipe calls for a pie crust filled with yellow cake dough, baked, cooled and covered with blackberry or raspberry jam then topped with heavy meringue and browned.

Which type did Mrs. Mary Cripps's students bake for the regents? The date would indicate a pie made from broken cake but that would mean the students had a supply of old cake or cake mistakes. This scenario is difficult to believe.

In this 1883 recipe for Washington Pie, the author states: "As there are other articles known by this name, it may be as well to state that this is a sort of brown bread pudding baked in a crust, such as is sold at the bakeries. Short paste is a plain pie crust made with flour, and butter, lard, drippings or minced suet."

The recipe is printed here exactly as it is in the 130-year-old book which suggests serving the pie with stuffed and baked beef heart and boiled navy beans.

WASHINGTON PIE ✤ ✤

From Chicago Herald Cooking School Book *(1883)*

1 pound of bread crumbs—
    a pressed-in quart
8 ounces of molasses or
    sugar—a teacupful
8 ounces of currants or raisins
2 teaspoons of mixed ground
    spices, chiefly cinnamon

1 teacupful of water
1 small cupful of vinegar
    or hard cider
8 ounces of suet chopped fine
2 eggs—optional

Mix everything together. Cover the bottom of a baking pan with a thin sheet of common short paste, pour in the mixture to be an inch and a half deep, cover with another thin crust, brush over the top with milk. Bake to a light color in a slow oven about three-quarters of an hour. Cut out squares either hot or cold.

Tea and Sweets

These cookies, and a vanilla version, were served on February 15, 2013, at Tea with Dean Virginia Moxley in Justin Hall's Hoffman Lounge. Friends, faculty, alumni, staff and students stopped by to help kick off K-State's 150th birthday celebration.

✤✤ LEMON ICEBOX COOKIES

From Practical Cookery *(1962)*

½ cup butter, softened	2 cups flour
1 cup sugar	1½ teaspoons baking powder
1 egg, well beaten	¼ teaspoon salt
1 tablespoon lemon juice	½ cup nuts, chopped
1 tablespoon grated lemon rind	

Cream butter and sugar together until fluffy. Add egg, juice and rind. Mix well. Combine flour, baking powder and salt. Stir into butter mixture. Stir in nuts. The dough will be stiff.

Divide dough into two equal pieces. Place each on wax paper and shape into neat rolls about 1½ to 2 inches in diameter. Wrap paper tightly around dough and pat until roll is smooth and even. Chill.

Preheat oven at 400°F. Unroll chilled dough and cut into ⅛-inch slices using a sharp knife and a sawing motion. Place slices on unoiled baking sheet and bake for 4 to 6 minutes.

YIELD: 80 COOKIES

Marshmallows may have gone gourmet in the 21st century but they predate almost all other confections. The marsh mallow plant grows in salty marshes. As long ago as 2000 B.C. in Egypt it was harvested for its sap and turned into a confection. In the medieval era pieces of the root were candied. In the 1800s, the juice extracted from roots was cooked with egg whites and sugar and hardened to become a medicinal candy to soothe sore throats. Gelatin replaced the sap but marshmallows weren't commercially available until about the time K-State was founded.

Many a kitchen on the edge of the frontier turned out marshmallows, taffy and other sweets when sugar became readily available. The Girl Scouts get credit for first publishing a recipe for what we now call s'mores. For Doretta Hoffman, dean of Human Ecology from 1954 to 1974, homemade marshmallows were a Christmas treat for the family. Most modern recipes use corn syrup.

DORETTA HOFFMAN'S MARSHMALLOWS ✤ ✤

2 (.25-ounce) envelopes
    unflavored gelatin
1½ cups water
2 cups sugar

Pinch of salt
1 teaspoon vanilla
½ cup finely ground nuts

Lightly butter a 9 x 9-inch square pan. Soak gelatin in ¾ cup water until dissolved. Boil sugar and the remaining ¾ cup water until it spins a thread (230–235°F on candy thermometer). Combine the two mixtures, let stand until partly cool. Add salt and vanilla and beat for about 15 minutes or until creamy and holds its shape.

Pour in the square cake pan and refrigerate. Cover with buttered waxed paper to keep from drying out. When set, remove by loosening edges, then drop upside down on buttered waxed paper. With a sharp damp knife, cut in pieces about 1 inch square. Roll each piece in finely ground nuts.

YIELD: 81 (1-INCH) MARSHMALLOWS

·2·
Bierocks
—— *and* ——
Boarding Houses

Recipes

THE TURN OF THE 20TH CENTURY WAS FRENETIC IN AMERICA:

- ❖ Chicago newspaperman L. Frank Baum published *The Wonderful Wizard of Oz*, forever changing the public image of Kansas;
- ❖ Henry Ford introduced the Model T, forever changing how people dined;
- ❖ The ice cream cone was introduced in 1904 at the Louisiana Purchase Exhibition in St. Louis;
- ❖ Milton Hershey invented Hershey Bars; John Harvey Kellogg introduced a new health food—Kellogg's Corn Flakes; James Dole canned his first pineapple.

In Manhattan, the little college on the hill threw off its training wheels and was on its way to becoming a food and food production powerhouse.

Nellie Kedzie's Biscuits

A young widow named Nellie Sawyer Kedzie was living in Topeka in 1882 when K-State President George Fairchild stopped by to visit alumnae in the area.

Nellie Sawyer graduated in 1876 and taught school in Milford and Ottawa for 5 years. She married Robert F. Kedzie and moved to Mississippi A & M College where he taught chemistry. When he died of malarial fever after less than 2 months of marriage, she moved back to Kansas.

Nellie Sawyer Kedzie, Class of 1876, was the first women to hold professor rank at K-State. One of her favorite sayings was "As the stream can flow no higher than its fountain, so no country can be better than its home."
COURTESY OF MORSE DEPARTMENT OF SPECIAL COLLECTIONS, KANSAS STATE UNIVERSITY LIBRARIES

"As was the custom, I invited [President Fairchild] to eat supper with us. As we were finishing the meal the president said to me, 'Do you think you can teach Kansas girls to make such biscuits as these we have just been eating?' It was a surprise question," she later wrote. "I answered, 'I could try.'"

"They were not looking for doctorates in those days; they wanted biscuits," she later wrote.

So the whirlwind that was Nellie Kedzie swooped into Manhattan, uprooting traditions and changing the college's direction, landscape and table. At her alma mater she became the first woman to hold the rank of professor, the first woman department head, the first woman to have a building named after her and was a nationally recognized pioneer in home economics.

Built in 1897, the Domestic Sciences Building, constructed with $16,000 from the begrudging legislature after Kedzie's personal lobbying efforts, is believed to be the first building in the world dedicated wholly to home economics. In 1902, it was renamed Kedzie Hall.

Kedzie wrote that she, along with the regents and Fairchild, decided that every girl who went through K-State should be taught hygiene, sewing and cooking (girls had to pass chemistry first). This was at a time when store-bought clothing was a novelty, when few people had iceboxes and when there was no power in the Farm Machinery Hall where the department was headquartered.

Most of the 1882 era recipes would have flabbergasted today's cook with instructions such as "take of flour the weight of 7 eggs" and no given oven temperatures.

Ovens did not have heat regulators or thermometers until 1916. Women used the age-old means of testing readiness. Hold a bare hand and arm in the oven and count to 20 before she was forced to pull out. That was a quick oven. She counted to 35 to 45 for moderate and 60 for slow.

The 1900 Domestic Science student cookbook, *Kansas Kook-Book for Kansas Kooks*, carried these instructions for testing oven temperature: "Paper Test for Oven: Tear off unprinted corner of a newspaper and place in small pan in oven. When it browns in 7 minutes it is the right temperature for sponge loaf cake, in 5 m. for butter loaf cake, in 4 m. for layer cake."

Biscuits, one of the few wheat flour breads with American origins, were baked in a quick oven.

Nellie Kedzie probably did not use a recipe for the biscuits she served President Fairchild. She probably served him standard baking powder biscuits, not flavored or fluffy or sweet. Her family moved to Kansas from Maine, so her mother most likely taught young Nellie to bake simple, hearty rounds made with butter or cream.

She left K-State in 1897. Remarrying in 1901, Nellie Kedzie Jones was a dominant force in home economics nationwide. When she retired to Smoky Hill Farm in Wisconsin, she wrote a column called "The Country Gentlewoman" for *Country Gentleman Magazine* from 1912 to 1918. It offered down-to-earth and good-humored advice to rural farmwomen. Her basic message was that a farm wife must spare herself in any small ways she could contrive so that she did not change into an overworked piece of farm equipment.

With that philosophy in mind, here is an updated biscuit recipe, one that requires a minimum of effort and a maximum of flavor, and does not turn the cook into an overworked piece of farm equipment.

Nellie Kedzie, standing left of post in 1888, taught classes in household economy, sewing, and cooking in Anderson Hall. Among her students in this class were Abby Lillian Marlatt and Anna Fairchild. The world's first building dedicated to domestic science education was built in 1898 and renamed Kedzie Hall in 1902. COURTESY OF MORSE DEPARTMENT OF SPECIAL COLLECTIONS, KANSAS STATE UNIVERSITY LIBRARIES

NELLIE KEDZIE'S BISCUITS UPDATED ✤ ✤

2 cups flour	½ teaspoon salt
1 tablespoon baking powder	¾ to 1 cup heavy cream
1 teaspoon sugar	

Preheat oven to 425°F.

In a large bowl, whisk flour, baking powder, sugar and salt. Add cream. Stir lightly to mix. If mixture is too dry, add more cream.

Turn onto lightly floured surface, knead several times to make smooth and pat to about ¾ inches thick. With a 2-inch round biscuit cutter, cut 12 circles. Gently reform scraps and cut more biscuits. Or cut into 12 squares. Place biscuits on cookie sheet and bake for 15 minutes or until golden.

Serve hot.

YIELD: 12 BISCUITS

The First Cooking Classes and the Birth of the Domestic Science Club

In 1874, John A. Anderson, the school's second president, divided the young college into three units: "farmer, mechanic and women's courses," then called household economy.

Anderson was eloquently and delightfully outspoken in his belief in the importance of educating women, even if that education concentrated on the "women's sphere."

He thought women had "a right to all the knowledge which related sciences can contribute to her intelligence, deftness and efficiency in the greatest and purest of womanly arts, the art of making homes brighter to the little ones than the streets, more attractive to its adults than saloons. These are things that men cannot perform."

Young women were never excluded from the educational vision at K-State or at Bluemont College. This idea was radical at the time when others preached about the evils of learned women and the problems that befall their frail constitutions when bombarded with such things as Latin and mathematics.

Cooking became part of the women's studies curriculum in 1876 when Mary E. Cripps organized a class for cooking instruction. Because the college had no

BRIGHT EYED AND VICTORIOUS

In 1908 the Kansas legislature mumbled about combining KSAC and the University of Kansas…or at least consolidating both engineering programs in Lawrence. This didn't sit happy with the administration in Manhattan or with the students.

The proud students took action: they invited legislators and their wives to come see what the college was doing. They raised more than $800 and rented a train to carry 285 visitors from Topeka to Manhattan on February 3, 1909.

Visitors toured barns, chapel, library and classes. They saw, *The Industrialist* reported, "4,000 eyes of the healthiest and brightest student body in the world." The domestic science class prepared and served dinner in Calvin Hall. More than 300 sat at a long table that stretched through the first floor of the building.

According to one report, "The legislators noticed that the food was a pleasing contrast to that [which] a Topeka restaurant had been furnishing them."

The consolidation issue never came up for a vote.

equipment for the new class, and because Mrs. Cripps was a milliner who taught sewing, she recruited faculty wives and townswomen who were "noted for their culinary art." The Assisting Society of Ladies guided the young students and helped equip the household economy kitchen laboratory.

Josephine Harper, a member of the class, remembered a lesson from Mrs. Geo. W. Higinbotham that involved soups. "I made the soup at home in the afternoon and took it to college the next morning in a tin pail with cups and spoons to serve the class at lesson." At a pie lesson, "Mrs. Purcell told us that cheese should be served with apple pie."

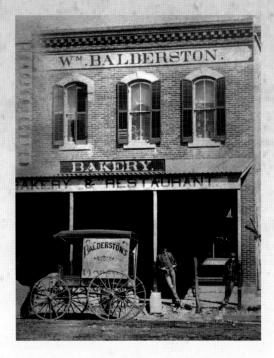

The Balderston Bakery, in the 200 block of Poyntz, made deliveries in a buggy around 1880. Courtesy of the Riley County Historical Society

The next year, Mrs. Cripps added a food course for third-year students who learned to make yeast bread and pastry.

The collaboration became the basis for the Domestic Science Club, still active today. Although minutes from 1882 are the first written records, the club notes its founding in the spring of 1876 with Mrs. Cripps as president and Mrs. E. M. Shelton as secretary. Among the first group were: Mrs. John Anderson, Mrs. M. L. Ward, Mrs. J. E. Platt, Mrs. E. B. Purcell, Mrs. N. A. Adams, Mrs. George S. Green, Mrs. Geo. W. Higinbotham and Mrs. Geo. C. Wilder.

As the college funded kitchen labs and kitchens and hired faculty to teach the food sciences, the Domestic Science Club focused on its members and the community. But it kept its historic and spiritual links to the College of Human Ecology.

Serious discussions—"Business Capacity of Women" and "Moral Bearings of Stanley's Explorations" in 1890, for example—mixed with teas and luncheons. During one early meeting Mrs. Purcell hosted an oyster supper at her home. "She served a five course luncheon, oysters several different ways and numerous other good things interspersed with music and laughter."

Louise Lanning, whose husband Francis taught chemistry, was president of the Domestic Science Club in 1965–66. Had she been around in 1876, Mrs. Cripps would have asked her to help teach the young students to cook. This is one of the many dishes for which Mrs. Lanning was known.

✤✤ BLUE HILL FUDGE CAKE
WITH COFFEE RUM ICING

From Louise Lanning

½ cup cocoa	½ cup sour cream
¾ cup strong coffee, hot	½ teaspoon baking soda
1 teaspoon vanilla	2 cups cake flour
½ cup butter or margarine	½ teaspoon salt
2 cups sugar	3 egg whites, beaten stiff

Preheat oven to 350°F. Grease and lightly flour two 8-inch round cake pans or a 9 x 13-inch pan. Shake out all loose flour.

Dissolve cocoa in coffee. Let cool. Add vanilla.

In a large bowl, cream butter and sugar. Add cocoa mixture. Mix sour cream with baking soda and add the butter mixture. Add flour and salt and beat well.

In separate bowl, beat egg whites until stiff but not dry. Fold into batter.

Transfer to prepared pans. Bake for 20 to 30 minutes or until done. Do not over bake.

Cool then frost with Coffee Rum Icing.

YIELD: 16 KANSAS-SIZED SERVINGS

COFFEE RUM ICING

6 tablespoons butter	4⅓ cups powdered sugar
6 tablespoons strong, hot coffee	1 teaspoon vanilla
	1 teaspoon rum extract

Combine butter and coffee. When cool, beat in sugar, vanilla and rum extract. If icing is too thin, add more sugar. It should be of spreading consistency.

Very Social Affairs

The Kansas State University Social Club formed in 1911. That year a trolley ran every 15 minutes carrying passengers from 4th and Poyntz to campus and KSAC enrollment had reached an astounding 2,335. The place was getting too darned big! So big that Margaret Waters, wife of the college's sixth president, organized a social club so women faculty members and faculty wives could be better acquainted. Dues were $1 and membership numbered 81.

The Social Club was active on campus and off. Members celebrated spring 1914 with a picnic supper. In 1921 they brought in Carl Sandburg to lecture. They held dances, card parties, art shows and outings such as the one to Kansas City for lunch and a play.

The mirror-image menu is from a 1912 senior-junior banquet on campus. COURTESY OF MORSE DEPARTMENT OF SPECIAL COLLECTIONS, KANSAS STATE UNIVERSITY LIBRARIES

They had tea in the president's home, a tradition that Noel Schulz, Kansas State's first lady and associate dean for research and graduate programs in the College of Engineering, continues today.

Since events meant refreshments, club members bought dishes so they wouldn't have to rent them from the local Duckwalls. They bought a silver tea service in 1925 for $74 and added other pieces along the way. The club silver is on display in the Alumni Center. Every year, club members gather to polish it.

At a gourmet dinner in 1983, the Social Club served this entree.

✤✤ PORK CROWN ROAST
WITH APRICOT STUFFING

From Virginia Ball

1 (5½ to 6-pound) pork rib
  crown roast (12 to 15 ribs)

1 tablespoon sugar

1 teaspoon instant chicken
  bouillon granules

¾ cup hot water

¼ cup diced dried apricots

4 cups dry, whole wheat
  bread cubes (about 5½ slices)

1 large apple, peeled, cored,
  and chopped

½ teaspoon finely shredded
  orange peel (orange zest)

½ teaspoon salt

½ teaspoon ground sage

¼ teaspoon cinnamon

⅛ teaspoon pepper

½ cup chopped celery

¼ cup chopped onion

¼ cup butter or margarine

¼ cup orange juice

1 tablespoon light corn syrup

½ teaspoon soy sauce

Preheat oven to 325°F.

Place roast, bone tips up, on rack in shallow roasting pan. Season with a little salt and pepper. Make a ball of foil and press into the cavity to hold it open. Wrap bone tips in foil.

Roast for 1½ hours.

To prepare stuffing, dissolve sugar and bouillon in hot water. Pour over apricots. Let stand for 5 minutes. In a large bowl combine bread, apple, orange peel, salt, sage, cinnamon and pepper.

Cook celery and onion in butter until tender. Add apricot mixture and bread mixture. Toss lightly to moisten.

Remove all foil from roast. Spoon stuffing lightly into the center, mounding high. Combine orange juice, corn syrup and soy sauce. Spoon over the meat.

Roast uncovered for 45 to 60 minutes, until meat thermometer registers 170°F. Baste occasionally with orange juice mixture.

YIELD: 8 TO 12 SERVINGS

Boarding and 'Batching'

Ivy Frances Harner was 15 and her brother Schuyler was 17 when they moved to Manhattan to start college in 1886. "We had practically exhausted the scholastic possibilities at our school," she wrote in her autobiography, *A Pioneer Girl*. She said her college wardrobe, except for hats and coats, was made at home or by the town dressmaker.

Her father traveled to Manhattan in the summer of 1886 to rent rooms for his son and daughter "to batch." She explained that meant they could do their own cooking. "You boarded if you could afford it, and you batched if you didn't board and with the abundance of food on our farm we could live better than those who boarded…"

After taking a break, Harner returned to KSAC and graduated as valedictorian in her class of 39 students in 1893. In her commencement address she said, "We are the children of yesterday, the learners of today and the burden bearers of tomorrow."

Two young women, perhaps K-State students, have tea in M. Zener's room at 1005 Humbolt in this undated photo from the historical society's Melton album. COURTESY OF THE RILEY COUNTY HISTORICAL SOCIETY

She earned a master's degree in 1897, helped start the school of home economics at Louisiana Technical Institute, then taught at Purdue.

The first college catalog, published for the 1863–64 school year, extolled the virtues of KSAC: "The location is very healthful. The water good, and air pure." But the college had no dormitories or dining facilities, so the catalog also explained where students could live and eat: "Students can get boarding in the city, including light and wood, in private families, for from $2.50 to $3.00 per week. Those who prefer it can rent rooms and board themselves much cheaper, perhaps at one-half the expense of boarding otherwise. For the convenience of those who may wish, a hack will carry students to and from the College, for $2 per term."

In 1875 when classes moved to a stone building in the present campus location, a student could get a room and meals for $2.75 a week, but the fee did not include fuel for the stove.

Boarding houses were lined up on the southeast corner of campus. There Aggieville sprang up to feed them and provide pencils, books, barbershops and laundries. Mrs. N. L. Haslam opened Bungalow Dry Good and Notions Store, at 631 North Manhattan, in 1911 to supply domestic science students with needs for sewing and cooking classes. Moro Street was paved in 1915.

Van Zile, the first student residence hall for women on campus, was not built until 1926. Men didn't move into a permanent residence hall until 1960. Later named Goodnow Hall, it housed 600 students.

Henriette Stewart was in her 80s when she befriended two students—Karla Hughes and Amelia Brown. She lived in their apartment complex on Kearney Street but had once run had a boarding house for graduate students with her late husband who was on the faculty.

"Mrs. Stewart fixed special treats for us after long days of studying," Hughes says. One of their favorites was this gingerbread.

MRS. HENRIETTE STEWART'S ✤✤
AGGIEVILLE GINGERBREAD

From Karla Hughes and Amelia Brown

½ cup sugar	½ teaspoon cinnamon
½ cup molasses	½ teaspoon ground cloves
¼ cup shortening, melted	½ teaspoon ground ginger
1 egg	1¼ cups flour
Pinch salt	½ cup hot water
½ teaspoon baking soda	¼ cup raisins, if desired

Preheat oven to 350°F. Grease an 8 x 8-inch baking pan.

Cream together sugar, molasses and shortening. Add egg and mix well.

In a separate bowl, combine salt, soda, cinnamon, cloves, ginger and flour. Stir half into the sugar mixture. Add water. Mix well. Add the rest of the flour mixture. Beat well. Add raisins if using.

Pour batter into prepared pan and bake for 20 minutes or until done.

YIELD: 9 SERVINGS

No Kitchen? No Boarding House? No Problem.

During the early part of the 20th century, eateries dotted the Manhattan landscape. Like today, K-Staters had their choices of plain or fancy. Unlike today, none of those choices involved chains. Fast food didn't involve drive-thru windows or eating en route. It meant sitting down, ordering, eating, and getting back to class quickly.

The Paddleford family, whose daughter would grow up to be one of K-State's most influential graduates, bought the Star Grocery Store in Manhattan in 1913. Clementine Paddleford graduated in 1921 but not before she had amassed a stack of menus and campus newspaper clippings including advertising aimed at college students.

Scrapbooks from her K-State years are part of her collection in the Hale Library Special Collection archives. They give us an idea of what students ate and where.

- ⚜ Harrison's advertised "Good Things to Eat." Paddleford wrote on the menus "the hangout for the gang" and "Johnie has cheated me out of ten gallon of ice cream since last fall." Harrison's served special steak (with potatoes, bread and butter) for 75 cents. But a tongue sandwich, or one made with cheese pimento, peanut butter or minced ham, was 10 cents. Shredded wheat was 10 cents as was pie and apple and celery salad. John Harrison first opened his grocery-tobacco-candy shop in 1904 at 11th and Bluemont.
- ⚜ The Pines Cafeteria advertised it was "the best place in town to eat." Mrs. Thomas Long was cafeteria director and L. C. Schafer the proprietor. Ads boasted of a dance hall upstairs that featured a special orchestra every Sunday.
- ⚜ J. L. Johns, 1123 Moro, offered "ice cream, sherbets, ices, confectionery of all kinds."
- ⚜ J. C. Dundore, who operated the Gold Medal Bakery at 1216 Moro, advertised "we have a clean, sanitary, well-lighted Bake Shop."
- ⚜ Georges College Candy Land, located in the Wareham Building at 412 Poyntz, advertised fountain specials and a selection of ice cream. One flavor was "brown bread."
- ⚜ The college canteen in the basement of Main Hall (Anderson) bragged about its soda fountain, complete luncheonette service, fruits and candies. Elmer Kittel was manager.

- Paddleford called Students' Inn at 708 North Manhattan Avenue, "the pie store."
- Colson's College Inn Café, Paddleford noted, was "the place for microbes and good looking men."

In the day before frozen everything, restaurants offered dozens of selections. Colson's listed eleven relishes, ten soups from ox tail to mulligatawny, six fish dishes, 21 listings under eggs and omelets and 41 listings under steaks and chops. They ranged from $2 for a porterhouse steak for two with mushrooms to two frankfurters with potato salad for 35 cents.

Menus were sprinkled with dishes made from all parts of the animal: fried honeycomb tripe, calves liver fried three different ways, calves brains and scrambled eggs, broiled sweetbreads, cold lamb's tongue, omelet with chicken livers. College Inn served Eggs Myerbeer, eggs and lamb's kidneys with a very thin white sauce.

Rex-Roy Café had a chef—Harry Quayle. He offered boiled leg of mutton with caper sauce for 40 cents, Veal *Cromeskies aux petite pors*, lobster with mushrooms au gratin and asparagus tips on toast. The restaurant at 302 Poyntz advertised it was open all night, to which Paddleford wrote in the menu, "Oh boy!"

Oysters were a winter habit in Kansas. They were shipped by the barrel, packed in seaweed and brine, from the Gulf of Mexico. One menu offered them 12 different ways. A dozen raw cost 50 cents, fried 60 cents.

In undated photo, "Miss Steele" drinks a bottle of grape juice for breakfast in the Manhattan area. COURTESY OF THE RILEY COUNTY HISTORICAL SOCIETY

❖❖ KEEBOBBED OYSTERS RORER STYLE

From Kansas Kook-Book for Kansas Kooks *(1900)*

> "50 large oysters, 1/2 c. minced celery or 2 tbs. dried celery, 1 pt. cracker crumbs, 4 eggs beaten light with 4 tbsp. milk, 1 tsp. salt, 1/8 tsp. white pepper, 1 tbsp. butter, 1 c. oyster liquid.

"Prepare the oysters according to the general rules. Dip each oyster into the egg mixture and then roll in cracker crumbs. Arrange a layer in a buttered baking dish. Then sprinkle with salt, pepper, celery and parsley. Dot with bits of butter. Then arrange another layer in the same manner, and so on, until the materials are all used up. Then sprinkle with cracker crumbs, and dot with bits of butter. Pour over this the oyster liquor which has been clarified. Bake about 20 m. Serve hot."

(Noted elsewhere in the KSAC book: "Clarify the liquor from oysters by heating until it is milky. Remove from stove and strain.")

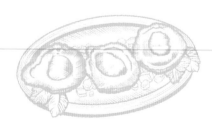

The First Training Table

The Manhattan YMCA set the first training table in 1908 when the Athletic Association added $1.50 to the $3 weekly board for athletes to ensure they "had ample supply of the most digestible and nourishing food." Later Mrs. Emil Thoes fed the athletes at her private boarding house.

Today, K-State Housing and Dining Services is responsible for the training table where giant-sized helpings of protein are cuisine of choice. But Monster Cookies are devoured with equal gusto.

A wagon advertises Purity Flour in the 200 block of Poyntz at about 1908. COURTESY OF THE RILEY COUNTY HISTORICAL SOCIETY

❖❖ MONSTER RECIPE FOR MONSTER COOKIES

From The Bakery at Derby Dining Hall

1 pound butter or margarine	11 eggs, lightly beaten
2 pounds granulated sugar	2½ teaspoons vanilla
(4½ cups)	2½ teaspoons baking soda
2 pounds brown sugar	18 cups quick oatmeal
(4 cups firmly packed)	1 pound M&M's or similar
1 tablespoon white corn syrup	candies
3 pounds peanut butter	1 pound chocolate chips
(6 cups)	(2⅔ cups)

Preheat oven to 350°F.

Cream butter, sugars, corn syrup and peanut butter until fluffy in an electric mixer. Add eggs and vanilla. Blend well. Stir in baking soda, oatmeal, candy and chocolate chips. Mix thoroughly.

Portion onto baking sheet with ½ cup measure. Flatten with palms. Bake for 12 minutes or until lightly browned.

Note: It may be necessary to put into dishpan to finish mixing by hand. However, the recipe may be halved with good results.

Yield: 8 dozen

Bierocks, Only in Kansas

Bierocks are the most famous Kansas food unheard of outside the state. Related to runzas and pirogi, bierocks are bread rolls filled with a beef/cabbage mixture. They are believed to have roots in Mennonite communities in Prussia, Lithuania and Ukraine.

As a senior in 2011, Brett Zeigler wrote that his family's bierock tradition came from his German great-grandparents. The Zeiglers immigrated to Kansas from Russia.

Janice Dinkel, associate professor of social work, grew up in Russell in a bierock-making family. Her "Aunt Butch" was the keeper of the family's Volga German recipe and made bierocks for many families in town.

Corrine Zorn got the nickname "Butch" when she was a child. She played basketball on the Gorham High School team and was often out in the yard shooting hoops and doing other traditionally "boy" activities. Aunt Butch, sister of Dinkel's mother Virginia, made dozens of bierocks each week, filling orders until she was well into her 70s. She even shipped them on dry ice to a transplanted Volga German in California.

"She was very secretive about the recipe and wouldn't share it with me even though I pleaded," Dinkel said. "I teased her once that after she died I would publish her cherished recipe right along with her obituary. Sometime soon after that the recipe appeared in my mailbox. Aunt Butch died May 20, 2002, and is missed by all who knew her."

Dinkel continues the family tradition, making dozens of bierocks every Christmas.

❖❖ DINKEL FAMILY BIEROCKS

From Corrine Zorn via Janice Dinkel

2 (¼-ounce) packages yeast (4½ teaspoons)	2 eggs, well beaten
6–6½ cups flour, separated	½ teaspoon salt
10 tablespoons sugar	½ cup plus 2 tablespoons butter, melted
2 cups warm water	Filling (recipe below)

Place yeast, 1 tablespoon sugar and ½ cup water (about 100°F) in a small bowl. Stir lightly. After 5 to 10 minutes, the yeast will form a foam on the water. It is ready to use.

In a separate bowl combine 2 cups flour, sugar, warm water, eggs, salt and butter. Stir in yeast mixture until well mixed.

Add 4 to 4½ cups flour to make a somewhat sticky dough. It should not be as stiff as typical bread dough. On a floured surface, knead until smooth and let rise until double, about 45 minutes.

Roll dough a little thicker than a pie crust. When ready to fill, cut in 5-inch squares. Place approximately 2 tablespoons filling in the center of each dough square. Pull corners to middle and pinch to seal. Place on ungreased cookie sheet, seam side down.

Bake at 375°F for 20 to 22 minutes or until the crust is golden brown. Brush with butter while cooling on rack.

YIELD: 24 BIEROCKS

BIEROCK FILLING

¾ of good-sized cabbage, shredded	Salt to taste
2 cups finely chopped onion	3 teaspoons black pepper
1½ pounds ground beef (85/15)	1 tablespoon garlic salt

Combine all ingredients in a large pan and cook until ground beef is browned and the vegetables are very soft. Make sure that the ground beef is fine in texture. Drain. Filling can't have much fluid in it when you put on dough.

Cool to room temperature before filling bierocks.

Eating from the Garden or the Can

For the K-State community, food continued to come from within 50 miles. But when folks couldn't eat with the season they turned to their own pantries and cellars, and to local merchants whose supplies came by boat or wagon.

Modern food processing began during the early 1800s with the invention of sealed jars for food. In 1825 Thomas Kensett of New York took out the first tin can patent. The Civil War spurred the need for canned foods. The first foods canned commercially in the United States were lobster and salmon, followed by corn, tomatoes, peas and beans. Those heading west avoided heavy cans on their journeys, but once settled they treated themselves to foods they couldn't get on the Kansas plains. Cowboys wrapped cans of tomatoes, sometimes costing more than $1 a can, in their bedrolls for both sustenance and liquid.

"Ruby was a good German girl who always brought something with vinegar in it when she came to visit us for dinner," writes Jocelyn Dunmire, who graduated in 1976. Her Great Aunt Ruby Scholz, from Frankfort, graduated with a degree in home economics in 1930 and was state director of the school lunch program for more than 30 years.

Ruby's younger sister Grace and brother Raymond were K-State grads as are Mrs. Dunmire's sisters Donna Blaske (BS and MS in education), Jennifer DeForest (MS in education) and Jeanette Jones Campbell (BS in agriculture). From Ruby Scholz's recipe box comes this salad:

AUNT RUBY'S GERMAN THREE BEAN SALAD ❖ ❖

From Ruby Scholz via Jocelyn Dunmire

---

1 cup sugar	1 (15.5-ounce) can kidney beans
1 cup vinegar	1 green pepper, diced
1 cup salad oil	1 small onion, diced
1 (15.5-ounce) can green beans	1 teaspoon celery seed or
1 (15.5-ounce) can yellow beans	mustard seed

Boil sugar, vinegar and oil until sugar is dissolved. Cool.

Drain and rinse beans. Place in large bowl and add green pepper and onion. Toss with dressing and celery or mustard seed.

Chill.

Warm fruit dishes served several roles on early Kansas tables—salad substitute, meat accompaniment, dessert. Scalloped recipes—such as pineapple casseroles and hot curried fruit—were popular in the 1950s and 60s.

Virginia Moxley, dean of Human Ecology from 2006 to 2013, is a fifth generation Kansan. Her ancestors have been in the territory since before K-State was founded. Her ranch cuisine reflects state traditions and the busy lives of the Moxley family. One recipe in her repertoire is the rhubarb sauce from a 1979 Council Grove community book called *Bell Ringing Recipes*.

✤✤ SCALLOPED RHUBARB

From Virginia Moxley

---

3 cups cubed stale bread,
    remove crusts and dice
    in ½ inch pieces
½ cup butter, melted

2 cups diced rhubarb
1 cup sugar
Red food coloring (optional)

Preheat oven to 325°F.

Mix bread and butter. Add rhubarb and sugar. Mix and put in 9 x 9-inch casserole dish. Add 1 tablespoon water plus a few drops of red food coloring to each corner if desired. Bake for 45 minutes.

YIELD: 6 SERVINGS

"Mother Bruce" and *"a fine loaf"* in an undated photo from the Melton photo album. COURTESY OF THE RILEY COUNTY HISTORICAL SOCIETY

Hot Meals

and

Cold Comfort

Recipes

THE GENERATION THAT FOLLOWED the settlers shared the values of their mothers and fathers—the land, commerce, the unwavering belief that human beings improved their lot through education.

In 1873, Kansans froze in a winter storm that lasted three days. Snow covered dugouts and filled log houses. The next year grasshoppers destroyed the spring wheat and corn. Grasshoppers again plagued Kansas in 1887 and in 1911. Kansas farmers moved from spring wheat to winter wheat.

The Hatch Act, passed in 1887, provided tax funds for agricultural research and the application of science became part of the culture of the family farm. In the 1910s, college entomologists stepped up with one solution: working with farmers they prepared 5,500 tons of mash to feed the grasshoppers. Recipe: 2,000 tons of bran, 100,000 gallons of syrup, 60,000 lemons and 100 tons of arsenic.

Grasshoppers and snowstorms were only some of the obstacles Kansans faced during the late 19th and early 20th centuries. Many tough times—from nature and manmade—were ahead. The Great Depression, the Dust Bowl and World War I marked the first half of the 20th century, all with palpable effect on K-State and the people it served.

K-State entomologist Hugh Thompson advocated using insects as food. He fed his students grasshopper cookies and deep-fried corn borers he claimed tasted like shrimp. According to one report, about half the class ate his insect cuisine. Thompson said their decisions did not affect their grades.

Today Gregory Zolnerowich, associate professor in entomology, carries on the Thompson tradition. He favors Chocolate Chirp Cookies that he serves in class and at K-State Open House each spring. "I don't do anything special for the cookies," he said. "I just use the basic recipe on the package of chocolate chips and add 100 to 120 roasted crickets to the cookie dough. It's pretty simple."

He notes that if one doesn't get excited about roasting crickets, cricket flour is available at some health food stores. This recipe is based on a favorite cookie at The Bakery and in the residence halls where the crickets are not included.

✦✦ CHOCOLATE CHIRP COOKIES

Adapted from K-State Dining Service's Chocolate Chunk Cookies

½ cup margarine	3 eggs, beaten
¾ cup plus 1 tablespoon shortening	4 cups flour
	1½ teaspoon baking soda
1¼ cup sugar	1½ teaspoon salt
1⅓ cup brown sugar	12 ounces chocolate chips
1½ teaspoons vanilla	1 cup chopped pecans
½ teaspoon water	100–120 dried roasted crickets

Preheat oven to 350°F.

Cream margarine, shortening, sugar, brown sugar, vanilla and water until sugars are dissolved. Blend in eggs well.

In smaller bowl, combine flour, baking soda and salt. Add gradually to creamed mixture, mixing well. Fold in chocolate chips, pecans and crickets.

Drop by tablespoons onto ungreased cookie sheet. Bake for 8 to 12 minutes or until light golden brown.

YIELD: 50 SERVINGS

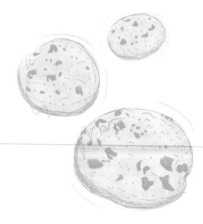

Extension and Food

"I was quite concerned about the amount of water women were carrying from wells, so I got to figuring how much it would cost to put a pitcher pump in the kitchen. I'll always remember Gladys Meyer (another specialist) telling about the time her mother was ill and her father carried water for a week. At the end of the week he came in and said, 'Now figure out where you want the sink and the bathtub because the plumber is coming out Monday morning,' and her mother said, 'It's too bad I didn't think to get sick long ago.' " Told by former Extension specialist Christine Wiggins to Ruth Hoeflin in *History of a College*.

Kansas State always took its land-grant mission seriously. The agricultural college sent its professors around the state on educational forays called Farmers Institutes.

The first was in 1868 in Manhattan. Professors talked about growing potatoes, Indian corn and fruit trees. In 1870, the institute added lectures on cheese making and wheat. That year Emma Haines Bowen, a member of the first graduating class in 1867, became the first woman to lecture at a Farmers Institute. Her topic: "The past, present and future of agriculture in our country."

In 1882, the little college conducted six institutes but as more students enrolled, the traveling classes became a greater burden in both time and money.

In those pre-automobile years, President E. R. Nichols persuaded the Chicago, Rock Island and Pacific Railway to foot the bill for Farmers Institute trains. In

A group of women are identified extension home economists in 1914. Courtesy of the Riley County Historical Society

1905 a train with two cars to serve as classrooms—one for wheat and one for corn—made 30-minute stops at 135 stations in two weeks.

The Board of Regents designated a Division of College Extension in 1912 and in 1914 the word "cooperative" was added when the 1914 Smith-Lever Act mandated federal funding for outreach. Between 1905 and 1937, at least 27 trains took information on agriculture and domestic economy to the people of Kansas so they could better feed their families and a growing world population. Fairs gradually replaced some functions of the institutes. County extension agents replaced other functions.

In the story of feeding Kansas, the extension service mirrors the state's history. Need to preserve garden produce? Extension folks will tell you safe canning procedures. Rural electrification made a home freezer possible? Extension folks will add freezing to their food preservation program. Their job was to spread food and nutrition knowledge, skills and practices and they took it seriously. When families bought radios in the 1920s, the KSAC instigated food-oriented programs. When health concerns became prominent, agents taught recipe modification.

Primary focus after nearly 150 years remains constant—producing food and getting healthy, safe, people-pleasing food on the table.

Much of the education was through women's groups called Home Demonstration Units after 1944 and Extension Homemakers Units after 1965. The first unit, a mother-daughter canning club, was created in 1914 in Leavenworth County and is one of the oldest extension units in the country.

When Gail Imig visited Kansas in 1976, the assistant director of national extension, commented: "I am very impressed with Kansas and that it is a friendly, warm and wonderful kind of state…Kansas Extension Homemakers Council is the kind of organization that is really the backbone of American Culture."

In *Cookie Classics*, Extension Specialists Karla Vollmar and Grace Lang presented the "cookies that made Kansas great." Lee Ann Schwartzkoph, a student, tested the recipes. This one listed under the category of Breakfast Brighten promises "a nutritious way to start your day!" You may prefer to use less sugar.

BREAKFAST BONANZA COOKIES ✦ ✦

From Kansas State University Cooperative Extension Service (1980)

6 slices bacon (or ¼ cup imitation bacon bits)	1 egg
	1 teaspoon vanilla
1 cup flour	¼ cup milk
½ teaspoon baking soda	3 cups quick-cooking oats
½ teaspoon salt	1 cup shredded sharp
⅔ cup margarine or butter	cheddar cheese
1 cup sugar	¼ cup wheat germ

Preheat oven to 350°F. Grease cookie sheets.

Fry bacon until crisp; drain, crumble and set aside. Combine flour, baking soda and salt. Set aside. Beat butter, sugar, egg, vanilla and milk together. Add flour mixture and blend thoroughly. Stir in oats, cheese, bacon and wheat germ.

Drop by teaspoon 2 inches apart on greased cookie sheets. Bake 8 to 10 minutes or until lightly browned.

Yield: 3 dozen

The long-running *Kids a Cookin'* series in the extension family nutrition program offered literature and videos in English and Spanish.

✤✤ DOG BONES

From Kids a Cookin'

½ **cup peanut butter**
(plain or chunky)
½ **cup instant nonfat**
dry milk powder

1 **tablespoon honey**
2 **tablespoons finely**
crushed graham
cracker crumbs

In large mixing bowl combine peanut butter and dry milk. Add honey and mix well. Divide dough into six pieces. Mold each piece into the shape of a dog bone. Sprinkle with graham cracker crumbs on both sides. Store in covered container in the refrigerator.

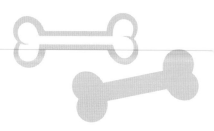

Head, Heart, Hands, Health and Appetites

Although 4-H membership has changed with the times—it is now mostly urban—no organization has touched as many lives in Kansas as has 4-H. 4-H members still learn about food, but today they tackle food safety, food science, smart food purchasing and food photography.

The first reference to youth work was in the November 1905 issue of the campus administration newspaper, *The Industrialist*. Henrietta Calvin, professor of domestic science, attended a Farmers Institute and reported, "There will be a Home Culture Club formed in Lincoln County by the young girls whose attention is to be devoted to the study of home questions and homemaking."

In 1906, Corn Clubs held competitions for farm boys between 12 and 18 years old. Each boy received a quart of seed corn from a local committee, planted it, cared for it, exhibited 10 ears and reported on his crop—number of stalks, number of ears, number of barren stalks.

Boys' and Girls' Experiment Clubs were started to study crop production and dairy (for the boys) and poultry and gardens (both boys and girls). Girls exhibited bread, cakes, pies, canned

Kansas 4-H conducted statewide Cherry Pie Baking Contests from 1950 through 1961. The winner went to a national competition in Chicago. The winners were announced over tea and cherry pie every year. Dates and identifications are not available. Courtesy of Morse Department of Special Collections, Kansas State University Libraries

This 1956 pattern for a 4-H dress cost 35 cents.
COURTESY OF DAVID MAYES, KANSAS STATE
UNIVERSITY DIVISION OF COMMUNICATIONS AND
MARKETING, K-STATE HISTORIC COSTUME AND
TEXTILE MUSEUM

fruits, jellies, sewing and embroidery at the county competitions.

4-H clubs were first formally listed in the 1926–27 college catalog. The clover symbolized "the importance and interdependence of development of head, hands, heart, and health," Julius T. Willard wrote in *History of the Kansas State College of Agriculture and Applied Science* in 1940.

Otis E. Hall, Kansas youth work director, wrote the 4-H pledge in 1918 but it was not adopted nationally until 1927. By 1930 Kansas had 625 clubs with 13,224 members and hundreds of 4-H leaders. Two of them were Mary Louise Anderson and Martha Streeter.

Mrs. Anderson grew up in Manhattan. She remembers eating Apple Brown Betty as a child at the K-State sponsored nursery school. Her mother, Belle Vlers Ficke, graduated in 1928. Martha M. Kramer, one of her professors, encouraged her and other students to apply for dietitian jobs at large hospitals in New York. "Mother was hired by Seaview Hospital on Stanton Island, New York, and later worked at Richmond Memorial, Princes Bay, Long Island," says Mrs. Anderson, Jamestown, Kansas.

As a K-State student, Mrs. Anderson took foods courses. She recalls, "Part of the training was to prepare a meal for guests and get everything timed so the food was ready when the guests arrived and we served it properly. That has been a very important lifelong skill for me. I love to entertain and like to do it properly. I was in Omicron Nu and when we had a banquet for initiation, crisp fried chicken was served. We all looked at that chicken and wondered how to approach it but I remembered that we learned in class that fried chicken was a finger food."

Mrs. Anderson taught foods to 4-H members for many years. A favorite with her pupils and her family was this recipe for Apple Crisp from the *Tricks for Treats Cookbook*. She still uses the recipe for apples and for rhubarb.

1 cup rolled oats (quick
cooking or regular)
½ cup sifted flour
½ cup brown sugar,
firmly packed
¼ teaspoon salt

1 teaspoon cinnamon
½ cup butter or
margarine, softened
4 cups peeled, sliced,
tart apples

Preheat oven to 350°F. Butter an 8 x 8-inch square baking dish.

Place rolled oats, flour, sugar, salt and cinnamon in the bowl and mix. Add soft butter or margarine and blend well with pastry blender or fork.

Arrange apples in prepared dish. Spread oatmeal mixture on top of apples and press down lightly.

Bake about 40 minutes or until topping is brown and apples are tender when tested with a fork.

Serve warm or cold with milk, cream or ice cream.

YIELD: 6 SERVINGS

4-H was such a big part of Martha Streeter's life that she had a green 4-leaf clover inset into the linoleum floor when she remodeled her Zeandale kitchen. She wrote about a 4-H demonstration she gave in the 1930s with Helen Stagg at the Topeka Free Fair after winning in Riley County. They were making an angel food cake and couldn't get the lid off the vanilla bottle. "After each of us tried it, we handed it to Dr. Lumb, the judge, and he opened it for us."

The next generation continued the 4-H demonstration tradition. Daughter Wreatha (now Tenny) and Joyce Vilander (now Plyer), members of the Zeandale 4-H Club, won twice at the state fair in Hutchinson, one time with this recipe.

❖❖ 4-H SANDWICH STROGANOFF
From Martha Streeter

1 teaspoon salt
1 pound ground beef
¼ cup chopped onion
¼ teaspoon garlic juice
¼ teaspoon black pepper
½ teaspoon Worcestershire sauce
2 tablespoons flour

¼ cup chili sauce
¾ cup sour cream
½ loaf French bread,
    sliced lengthwise
Garnishes: grated cheese, sliced
    tomatoes, green pepper rings

Add salt to pre-heated skillet. Brown beef and chopped onion. Add garlic, pepper and Worcestershire sauce. When meat is cooked, stir in flour, then chili sauce. Reduce heat and blend in sour cream. Spoon onto bread and garnish.

Broil until cheese is melted and serve immediately.

YIELD: 4 SERVINGS

Merle Eyestone's 4-H career lasted more than 70 years from club member, agent and leader to director and benefactor. He was raised in Lansing and got a degree in agricultural economics in 1947. He retired as executive director of the Kansas 4-H Foundation.

TEN-BEAN SOUP ❖ ❖

From Merle Eyestone
Published in Essence of Kansas! Taste--:
Food Experiences with 4-H Friends *(1988)*

1 pound mixed dried beans	1 (16-ounce) can diced
2 cups chopped ham	tomatoes
2 quarts water	1 teaspoon chili powder
1 large onion	1 minced garlic clove

Combine beans with water and cover. Soak overnight. Drain. Combine beans and ham with 2 quarts water and cook 2½ to 3 hours. Add remaining ingredients. Simmer 30 minutes. Season to taste with salt and pepper.

YIELD: 10 SERVINGS

❖❖ WHEAT CASSEROLE

From Coralee Thornburg
Published in Essence of Kansas! Taste--:
Food Experiences with 4-H Friends *(1988)*

2 cups cooked wheat (bulgur)	1 tablespoon instant minced onion
1 (10-ounce) can mushroom soup	1 cup (4 ounces) American cheese, shredded
½ cup sour cream	1 cup crushed potato chips
	2 ounces chopped pimento

Preheat oven to 350°F. Grease 8 x 8-inch baking dish.

Combine cooked bulgur, soup, sour cream, onion and cheese. Pour into prepared dish. Bake 1 hour. Remove from oven and stir. Top with chips then sprinkle with pimento and bake for 10 more minutes.

Yield: 8 servings

FLINT HILLS BEEF SALAD ✤✤

From Brenda and Ginger Wessel
Published in Essence of Kansas 4-H Cookbook *(1994)*

½ cup olive oil

3 tablespoons tarragon vinegar

1 tablespoon Dijon mustard

1 teaspoon dried tarragon

1 teaspoon salt

2 pounds boneless sirloin steak

1 head cauliflower, cut into
flowerets

1 head broccoli, remove
stalks, chopped

¼ cup milk

1 each red and yellow bell
pepper, chopped

1 medium red onion,
thinly sliced

½ cup crumbled crisp-fried
bacon

1 cup grated Parmesan cheese

1 head lettuce, torn

Combine oil, vinegar, mustard, tarragon and salt in container with tight lid.
Shake to mix well. Chill for several hours.

Cook steak as desired to at least medium-rare. Cut into cubes. Combine
with cauliflower, broccoli, milk, bell peppers, onion and bacon in large bowl.
Mix well then chill for 1 to 2 hours.

Shake dressing, then add to beef mixture. Add cheese and toss to mix well.
Place lettuce on serving plates and mound beef mixture in the center.

YIELD: 8 SERVINGS

'KANSAS—Say it above a Whisper'

The legendary Mamie Alexander Boyd believed in Kansas, she believed in community and she believed in K-State. Her stationery was engraved with the words: Kansas—say it above a whisper.

Mary Emma "Mamie" Alexander was born in 1876 and grew up on a farm near Humbolt. Her autobiography, *Rode a Heifer Calf Through College*, chronicles a Kansas life with distinction and humor. The book title comes from the fact that she sold her calf for $17.50 to finance her first year at KSAC.

Mamie Alexander, Class of 1902.
COURTESY OF MORSE DEPARTMENT OF
SPECIAL COLLECTIONS, KANSAS STATE
UNIVERSITY LIBRARIES

In 1902 she graduated in printing and general science and was president of the senior class. In college she met Frank W. Boyd whom she married in 1905. They had two sons, George McDill "Huck" Boyd and Frank W. "Bus" Boyd Jr. The *Phillips County Review* was their first of several newspapers, and Mamie continued to publish it after her husband's death in 1947.

Mamie Boyd was elected the first woman president of the KSU Alumni Association in 1930 and president of the National Federation of Press Women in 1940. She received Kansan of the Year, Outstanding Newspaper Woman of Kansas and Kansas Press Woman of the Year honors and the K-State distinguished service award in journalism in the 1950s.

In the 1960s, she was named Kansas Mother of the Year, won the National Newspaper Association's McKinney Award, became the first woman to receive the William Allen White Foundation award for journalistic merit and had a KSU residence hall named after her. In 1963 she was chosen Homecoming Centennial Queen for the university's 100th anniversary. She rode in a 1909 "Reo" car dressed in an 1885 outfit of a bustled, draped skirt of black alpaca and a plumed hat.

Mamie, Frank Sr., Huck and Frank Jr. were all inducted into the Kansas Newspaper Hall of Fame. The Huck Boyd National Center for Community Media and the Huck Boyd National Institute for Rural Development at KSU were later established in memoriam of her eldest son.

She credited her energy and achievements to the fact that, "When I work, I work hard; when I sit down, I sit down easy, and when I worry, I go to sleep."

Most of that energy went into newspapering but she knitted constantly and found time to make jelly and pickles.

Recipes from Mamie Boyd and her daughter-in-law Marie Kriekenbaum Boyd, who married Huck in 1930, were contributed by Anne Krauss Brockhoff, Mamie's great-granddaughter and Huck's granddaughter; Mary Beth Boyd, who is married to Mamie's grandson, Dick Boyd; and Ginny Dunkelberger, Marie Boyd's niece. "I don't believe cooking was her top priority," recalls Mary Beth Boyd about her great aunt. "She loved the newspaper business, K-State, her family and friends, clubs and community service. I do remember that she enjoyed making jelly during the summer and giving it away for gifts."

MAMIE BOYD'S RED APPLE SALAD ✤ ✤

⅓ cup Red Hots candy	1 (3-ounce) package red gelatin
1 cup boiling water	2 cups applesauce

Dissolve Red Hots in water, then add gelatin. Stir until gelatin is dissolved. Cool slightly. Stir in applesauce. Cool and serve.

YIELD: 4 SERVINGS

MARIE BOYD'S RED BEEF BRISKET ✤ ✤

1 cup beef broth	Black pepper
3 tablespoons vinegar	Garlic, if desired
3 tablespoons soy sauce	5 or 6 pound beef brisket

Combine broth, vinegar, soy sauce, pepper and garlic. Add brisket. Let stand in sauce overnight in the refrigerator. Bake at 250°F for 5 or 6 hours or until tender.

War Food Administration posters during World Wars I and II encouraged Americans to increase food production and conservation. Kansas State University stepped in to help farmers, stockmen and homemakers increase yields and learn food preservation, gardening and meatless-sugarless cooking. POSTER CREATED BY DICK WILLIAMS, UNITED STATES DEPARTMENT OF AGRICULTURE, 1944.

Anne Brockhoff says this is one of her mother's signature recipes. Mayonnaise cake was probably developed during the Great Depression as an economic substitution for milk and butter. Mrs. Krauss (granddaughter of Mamie and Frank Boyd Sr. and daughter of Huck and Marie) graduated from K–State in 1959.

MARCIA BOYD KRAUSS'S CHOCOLATE ✤✤ MAYONNAISE CAKE

2½ cups sugar

6 tablespoons cocoa

2 teaspoons baking soda

1½ teaspoons salt

1 cup mayonnaise

1½ teaspoons vanilla

2 eggs

3 cups all-purpose flour

2¼ cups boiling water

Preheat oven to 380°F. Butter and flour a 9 x 13-inch cake pan.

Combine sugar, cocoa, baking soda and salt in a large bowl. Combine mayonnaise, vanilla and eggs in a small bowl; combine with sugar mixture and mix well.

Add flour and boiling water (alternate between the two as you mix) and blend thoroughly and quickly.

Pour into prepared cake pan and bake for 10 minutes. Lower heat to 350°F and bake another 25 minutes or until a toothpick comes out clean. Cool completely, remove from pan if desired and then frost with your favorite chocolate icing.

YIELD: 15 SERVINGS

·4·

The Land of Steak
──── *and* ────
Pie

Recipes

THE PERFECT MEAL? "Steak and cherry pie," one Kansas farmer answered. Meat and pie. It was true 150 years ago. It is true today.

Look at any food map of the United States. Smack in the middle will be a steak or a steer and wheat stocks or a loaf of bread. Meat and wheat—Kansas powerhouses fueled by Kansas State University scientists.

"…with bread in hand"

Don Isaac and Connie Wiebe Isaac, graduates of Tabor College in Hillsboro, lived in Jardine Terrace in 1963 and 1964 when he was earning a master's degree in agricultural economics. She worked at the library.

"We ate Vienna sausages wrapped in biscuit dough and ham hock-navy bean soup," Connie Isaac recalls.

Years later they returned to Tabor when Don joined the faculty and she coordinated the Learning in Retirement program. There, in the historic heart of Kansas wheat country, he bakes bread.

"There are a number of characteristics of bread bakers that make them unique people in the world," Don Isaac wrote several years ago for a college convocation.

"A bread baker always lives in a community with others. You don't bake bread by yourself; you share with family, the neighbor down the street, or the church potluck. A bread baker is inherently optimistic and intimately involved in doing something with hands and simple materials to help others. When I meet my neighbor with bread in hand, I don't have room for a stick, or rock, or a missile."

How Kansas Became America's Breadbasket

One story about the state's journey to being the Wheat King goes like this:

Anna Barkman was 8 years old when her father, Peter, decided to move the family from their Volga German Mennonite community in Russia to Kansas. The Barkmans were one of the 35 Mennonite families that settled in central Kansas in Marion County in 1874. The leader of the church group was Jacob A. Wiebe, Connie Isaac's great uncle.

Other Mennonites were already in the state but this was the first entire community to move. They re-formed their old world village and congregation and called it Gnadenau (meaning meadow of grace).

According to the story she told later, Anna's job was to separate 2 gallons of the finest kernels of Turkey red hard winter wheat, a strain developed in Turkey that grew well on Ukrainian farms, for the journey.

An estimated 10,000 Mennonites came to the prairies between 1873 and 1884. Like the generations of wheat farmers that followed, the Barkmans were resilient, flexible, reliable, imaginative. Their farming practices and their seed wheat worked well in Kansas.

Bernard Warkentin built a mill in Halstead to process the wheat. Many give him credit for making Turkey red wheat available to other farmers.

Kansas farmers grew hard winter wheat on only about ⅓ acre per person in the family. That was enough to keep them in bread and cakes until the next harvest.

As technology advanced, rural families moved toward a market economy. Farmers needed money to buy tractors to replace horse-drawn plows and thrashers to replace scythes. So they grew more hard winter wheat. Wheat became a cash crop and flour, after grist mills were converted from stone burrs to steel rollers that could handle the harder grain, became a commodity shipped by railroad out of Kansas and into homes and bakeries around the country.

Kansas became known as the Wheat State, the nation's breadbasket. Today it grows more wheat than any other state, nearly 20 percent of all produced in the United States. Almost all Kansas wheat grown is hard red winter wheat.

The transition from spring-planted soft wheat to hard winter wheat was an important one for Kansas and for Kansas State University.

In March 1863, a month after the college was established, J. S. Hougham, the first professor of agricultural science, sowed spring wheat in the college's first wheat experiment. By 1880, researchers were trying to hybridize wheat perfect for the state's harsh climate and damaging diseases.

Typically Kansas farmers produce more wheat than any other state in the nation. In 2011, the state also ranked first in wheat flour milling daily capacity. In the 2007 census, Kansas recorded 65,531 farms. COURTESY OF DAVID MAYES, KANSAS STATE UNIVERSITY DIVISION OF COMMUNICATIONS AND MARKETING

Since the early 1900s, the K-State wheat-breeding program has released 42 wheat varieties, each a step forward in resistance to disease, quality and/or increased yields.

In 1998, 75 percent of a 494.9 million bushel wheat crop was planted in hard winter wheat developed by K-State. In 100 years, average yield had risen from 14.5 bushels an acre to 49 bushels an acre. In Kansas, the average dollar value per year for wheat production between 2007 and 2012 was $2.101 billion.

KSAC-training agronomists traveled the world looking for seed stock. They were called plant explorers, hired by the United States Department of Agriculture to search for plants of potential use in the United States.

One of the most famous was David Fairchild who, at age 22, created the Section of Foreign Seed and Plant Introduction. He spent 37 years visiting every continent (except Antarctica) and returning with hundreds of plants that included alfalfa, soybeans, mangos and pistachios. The son of KSAC president George T. Fairchild, he graduated in 1888. He was married to Miriam Graham Bell, daughter of Alexander Graham Bell.

Another famous plant explorer was M. A. Carleton who was an 1887 graduate and faculty member. He introduced rust-resistant hard red wheat to the American Wheatbelt, including Crimean, the parent of the first improved varieties that K-State developed. One plant historian wrote that in 1919, "it may not have been an exaggeration to say that 98 percent of wheat grown in Kansas came from Carleton's seed stock."

At one time Carleton tried to convince farmers to grow durum wheat, commonly called macaroni wheat. He collected European chefs' recipes for croquettes, spaghetti, vermicelli and more to publish in a bureau of plant industry bulletin.

Into the Kitchen

The first settlers planted corn. It grew fast, could feed family and livestock and didn't take lots of space or equipment. From American Indians, the newcomers learned about corn, an important New World plant along with tomatoes, potatoes, chocolate and vanilla (from an orchid plant).

But European settlers did not fall in love with bread made from corn. They wanted wheat flour like they had in Europe and the whiter the better.

Hard winter wheat, planted in the fall and harvested in early summer, thrived in the Kansas climate and soil. And it thrived in the kitchen. Its high protein and strong gluten structure made it ideal for the yeast breads a growing population craved.

THE SEED COMPANY BROTHERS

In Atchison, the Prussian-born August Mangelsdorf founded the Mangelsdorf Brothers Seed Company in the 1870s. It became one of the premier seed companies of the era. Two of his sons studied agronomy at K-State, Albert J. graduating in 1916 and Paul C. in 1921.

Paul Mangelsdorf discovered the genetics and origin of corn before retiring from a distinguished career at Harvard University. He received an honorary doctor of laws degree from K-State in 1961 for his contributions to agriculture and society. "He was not only a researcher and plantsmen, but also a humanitarian deeply interested in the lives of poor farmers everywhere in the world," wrote biographer Kenneth Thimann.

Albert Mangelsdorf earned a doctorate at Harvard then headed west. He is recognized worldwide for helping make sugarcane a successful major crop in Hawaii.

Bread flour is made from hard winter wheat. Varieties with weaker gluten and lower protein are milled into all-purpose flour.

In the 1970s, wheat scientists started working on white winter wheat, used for yeast bread, hard rolls, tortillas and noodles. Labeled white whole wheat flour in stores, the flour is milled from the whole wheat berry so it is more nutritious than bran-less, germ-less, regular wheat flour. The first released by the Kansas Experiment Station in 1998 was called Keyne.

The latest wheat breed, approved for release in 2013 after 10 years of testing, is named in honor of the founding of K-State. It's called 1863.

K-State wheat breeder Allan Fritz called it a medium maturity variety that has good resistance to soilborne mosaic virus and good soil acid tolerance. But importantly for home and commercial bakers, it makes good bread flour.

Becky Miller tested 1863 at the K-State Wheat Quality Lab she directs. She believes it promises good things for Kansas. "1863 meets the quality needs of producers, millers and bakers while at the same time carrying on the tradition and quality of the K-State wheat breeding program."

Recipe developers put the work of the scientists and farmers in the kitchen and then on the table. One recipe was created by dining service's Fern Mayfield and Sarah Severns and Coila Farrell, a hospitality management graduate who executed the recipe at the California Raisin Marketing Board's America's Best Raisin Bread Contest competition and won third place in the nation in 2009.

GOLDEN HARVEST RAISIN ✧✧
BREAD WITH WALNUTS

From Coila Farrell

⅓ cup walnuts, coarsely
chopped

½ cup golden raisins

½ cup dried cranberries

1 cup water (120–130°F)

4 to 5 cups bread flour,
divided

2 tablespoons yeast

1 egg, lightly beaten

⅓ cup brown sugar

6 tablespoons unsalted
butter, softened

2 teaspoons salt

1 cup mashed sweet
potatoes

Preheat oven to 350°F. Spread chopped walnuts on baking pan, toast for 5 minutes. Cool to room temperature.

Place raisins and cranberries in a bowl. Cover with lukewarm water and allow to plump for 15 minutes. Drain well.

In a mixer bowl, place 1 cup bread flour and yeast. Mix for 30 seconds to combine. Pour in water and mix at medium speed for 2 minutes or beat 100 strokes.

Attach dough hook if you have one. Add egg, brown sugar, butter, salt and sweet potatoes. Slowly add bread flour ¼ cup at a time until dough is clearing sides and bottom of mixing bowl. If using a dough hook, knead on medium speed for 8 to 10 minutes, until dough is smooth. Or knead by hand until dough is smooth.

Add walnuts and raisin/cranberries, kneading until they are well incorporated. Place dough in greased bowl, cover and let rise until double, 1 to 1½ hours.

Shape dough into 2 loaves. Place in greased 9 x 5 bread pans. Cover with plastic wrap that has been spritzed lightly with pan spray. Let rise until doubled, approximately 1 hour.

Preheat oven to 350°F. Bake loaves for 20 minutes. Cover loaves with foil; continue to bake for an additional 20–25 minutes until loaves are golden brown and sound hollow when tapped on the bottom.

YIELD: 2 LOAVES

Is Your Flour Made with Kansas Wheat?

If you live in Kansas, it probably is, says Becky Miller, director of K-State's Wheat Quality Lab.

Transportation is expensive so mills typically source their wheat close to home. There are flour mills in Kansas City, Hutchinson, Stafford County (Hudson flour) and Marienthal (Heartland Mill). King Arthur white whole wheat flour is milled near Salina.

It's hard to know how much of the new 1863 variety will be grown. "But definitely it will make it to the home baker, and also to industrial domestic bakers and international bakers, too," she said. About half of Kansas wheat is exported.

Norman Saul wrote that Kansas wasn't really the wheat state, it was the flour milling state. At the turn of the century 533 mills turned wheat into flour.

The university's milling tradition began in 1906 when researchers in cereal chemistry asked questions about milling qualities of different wheat varieties. The milling industry department was established in 1910 and grew into a milling curriculum in 1917. In 1918 K-State was the only college in the world offering a degree in flour milling engineering.

From agronomy classrooms and researchers grew the Kansas wheat industry, 1934. COURTESY OF MORSE DEPARTMENT OF SPECIAL COLLECTIONS, KANSAS STATE UNIVERSITY LIBRARIES

On Wednesdays during fall and spring semesters, a steady parade streams into Shellenberger Hall buying flour and bulgur from the Milling Science Club and cookies and bread from the Bakery Science Club. Their operation is called Sweet Memories and, indeed, the student bakers' products hold dear places in the hearts of graduates.

When she was a senior, Maddy Beck earned first place in the commercial division of the student competition of the fourth annual America's Best Raisin Bread Contest. Beck's winning entry was Barbecue Raisin Bread. "I wanted to create a new flavor profile for raisin bread," she explained. "During my internship at Caravan ingredients, I was inspired by Kansas City BBQ. What better than BBQ raisin bread!" Beck graduated in 2012 in food science and industry.

Most grocers carry barbecue spice mix. Choose one that does not have salt or sugar as the first ingredient if possible. The barbecue flavor is subtle so you might want to add more or less depending on the spice you choose and your taste. The recipe was tested also using half white bread flour and half whole wheat flour.

BARBECUE RAISIN BREAD ✤ ✤

By Maddy Beck

Adapted for home use using bread machine

1⅓ cups water	3 tablespoons sugar
4 cups bread flour	1 tablespoon barbecue
2 tablespoons butter	spice blend
1 teaspoon salt	1½ cups raisins
2 tablespoons dry milk	3 teaspoons yeast

Place ingredients into bread machine pan in the order suggested by the manufacturer. Select large loaf setting. When bread maker indicates, add raisins. Continue according to manufacturer's directions.

YIELD: 1 2-POUND LOAF

❖❖ WHOLE WHEAT SUGAR COOKIES
Adapted from Food for Fifty *(2001)*

The original recipe calls for whole wheat flour. I substituted white whole wheat flour, available at most grocery and natural food stores, and milled for King Arthur Flour from Kansas hard white winter wheat.

1 cup margarine or butter	2 teaspoons baking powder
2¼ cups sugar, plus 5 tablespoons for topping	1 teaspoon baking soda
	1 teaspoon salt
2 eggs	1 teaspoon ground nutmeg
2 teaspoons vanilla	2 tablespoons grated orange peel
¼ cup milk	
4 cups whole wheat white flour	1 teaspoon ground cinnamon

Preheat oven to 375°F. Prepare baking sheets by lining with parchment paper or greasing lightly.

Cream margarine and 2¼ cups sugar together for 5 minutes or until light and fluffy. Add eggs, vanilla and milk and mix well. In a separate bowl, combine flour, baking powder, baking soda, salt, nutmeg, and orange peel. Mix then gradually add to creamed mixture. Blend well.

In a small bowl combine 5 tablespoons sugar and cinnamon. Drop by tablespoonful on prepared pan and flatten slightly. Sprinkle with sugar-cinnamon mixture and bake for 8 to 10 minutes.

YIELD: 4 DOZEN

Feeding the Kansas Wheat Crew

Growing up on a farm in the 1950s, wheat harvest was a special time. When I was very young, I remember my mother driving the old family station wagon to the wheat field to take Dad (John C. Pretzer, 1941 graduate in animal husbandry) lunch and lemonade. He didn't like a lot of ice because, he said, it just made him hotter later in the afternoon. But I remember him pouring water from the jug over his head, both to cool off and to float away wheat chaff. No protective air-conditioned cabs on his combine. He pulled it behind his International Harvester "H" tractor. On extra hot days he put up an umbrella.

When I was a little older and my dad farmed more land, the neighbors pitched in, driving trucks and second combines. Then my sister, Mother and I spent the morning making dinner (the noon meal) for the crew. We dressed and fried chickens (which Dad had beheaded before he left for the field because that was one of the only farm tasks Mother refused to do), snapped green beans, peeled potatoes and made dessert—one that went with ice cream. The dust-covered men crowded around the table with the family in the hot kitchen. I remember the heaping platters of food quickly emptied. I remember lots of conversation and laughter. I remember happiness. The men—they were probably teenagers—were polite and appreciated our morning's work.

When I was old enough to manage the lumbering ancient 1947 Chevy dump truck, I drove loads of wheat to the Elmdale elevator. In good years, my dad was delighted to get $2 a bushel for wheat. Last year, my brother Charles Pretzer, who still farms that rich Cottonwood River bottom land, remembers the price as high as $8 and yields in the 60 bushels an acre range.

I still associate hard work with sweat, good times and good food.

This is how Clementine Paddleford reported to the world that chicken was fried in Kansas. It is how my mother did it and how I still do it. Mother added a quick step, although it would make food safety folks cringe today. She put salt, pepper and flour in a brown paper grocery sack, put the chicken pieces in the sack, and shook it to coat each piece and help it shed excess flour.

Directions for Paddleford's chicken are written exactly as they were printed in her 1960 book, *How America Eats*. Paddleford first wrote the chicken recipe in a 1942 column in *This Week* magazine. In "Let's Have an Old-fashioned Fourth!" she recreated a 1912 Kansas picnic (Box 64 Folder 151 of the Paddleford Papers).

❖❖ HONEST-TO-GOODNESS KANSAS FRIED CHICKEN

From Clementine Paddleford

---

8 chicken pieces or 1 (2½ to
   3-pound) broiler chicken
   cut into pieces
2 tablespoons unsalted butter
4 tablespoons lard (vegetable
   shortening)

Kosher salt and freshly ground
   black pepper, to taste
2 cups hot milk, plus more
   if needed
⅔ cup all-purpose flour

Preheat the oven to 200°F. Wash the chicken pieces and pat them dry with paper towels. Season them generously with salt. Season the flour with a little salt and pepper. Roll the chicken pieces in the flour and pat evenly with your fingertips. Reserve any leftover flour for the gravy.

Melt the butter and lard in a large, heavy skillet over medium heat. When hot but not smoking, add the chicken, largest pieces first. If the skillet won't hold 8 pieces in one layer with room for turning, fry in batches, grouping white and dark meat separately so the white meat stays juicy. Partially cover the skillet so the fat doesn't splatter but the chicken doesn't steam. As chicken pieces brown, turn them. White meat will be finished when the meat close to the bone is light pink: dark meat will be finished when cooked through and fork-tender.

When the chicken is ready, drain it on a rack set in a baking pan. Put the pan in the warm oven while you make the gravy: Pour off all but 2 to 3 tablespoons of fat in the skillet and whisk in 2 tablespoons of the remaining seasoned flour. Cook over medium-low heat for about 1 minute, until the mixture begins to bubble. Then slowly add the hot milk and heat the gravy, whisking constantly, until thickened, about 5 to 7 minutes. For a thicker gravy, continue cooking for a few extra minutes; for a thinner gravy, add more milk. Season the gravy with salt and pepper and serve over the chicken.

YIELD: 4 SERVINGS

NOTE: *When the chicken has cooled, lay the pieces in a big bread pan padded with paper towels. Cover with a tea towel, a la 1912. When the towel is lifted there is chicken in a golden pyramid, piece upon piece, crisp but not crackly, the soft meat finely grained under the coating. Thin slices of homemade yeast bread and plenty of butter are the things to eat with fried chicken. And pass crisp chunks of watermelon pickles—it adds that something special. As do quince preserves.*

Ode to the Watermelon Pickle

My Grandmother Flora Pretzer, who was born in 1895, never wasted a tablespoon of food. She traded potato peelings to the chickens for eggs. She made pickles from watermelon rinds—they were summer in a jar.

Her watermelon pickles were on every holiday table. She would only use Black Diamond watermelon because she said they had the best rind. Watermelon eaters and growers might like the modern varieties that have more red fruit and thinner rind. But pickles suffer.

GRANDMA PRETZER'S WATERMELON PICKLES ✤ ✤

By Flora Pretzer

5 pounds watermelon rind	1 tablespoon black pepper
1 tablespoon alum	1 cup vinegar
4 cinnamon sticks	3 pounds sugar (6 cups)
1 tablespoon whole cloves	10 ounces maraschino cherries
1 tablespoon whole allspice	

The rind is the white of the watermelon. Trim all the pink and, of course, the dark heavy skin. Rinds should be at least an inch thick. Cut into ½ by 1½ -inch pieces.

Boil rind for 1 hour. Add alum and boil for ½ hour more.

Meanwhile tie cinnamon, cloves, allspice and pepper in a spice bag or muslin. Add to vinegar and sugar. Boil 30 minutes. Add rind and boil for additional 10 minutes. Add cherries.

Put into sterilized pint jars. Add one cinnamon stick and a few cherries to each jar and fill with syrup leaving ¼ inch space at the top. Seal.

YIELD: 3 TO 4 PINTS

Pie: The Other Half of Dinner

Barbara Swell is related to K-State via her son, Wes Erbsen, who is doing graduate work in physics. The author of 10 historic cookbooks including *Log Cabin Cooking* and *The Lost Art of Pie Making*, the North Carolina food historian and cooking teacher is currently working on a pie crust book. She agreed to share her favorite. One of her secrets: make the pie crust the day before you bake.

Even in the early K-State classroom, pie was on the Kansas menu, undated. COURTESY OF MORSE DEPARTMENT OF SPECIAL COLLECTIONS, KANSAS STATE UNIVERSITY LIBRARIES

BASIC FLAKY BUTTER PIE CRUST ✢ ✢

From Barbara Swell

2½ cups all-purpose flour
Scant 1 teaspoon fine salt
1 cup (2 sticks) cold unsalted
butter

2 teaspoons lemon juice or
cider vinegar stirred into
½ cup ice cold water

Combine flour and salt in a bowl. Cut the butter into ½ inch cubes. Divide the cubes into two piles. Add one pile of cubes to your flour mixture and blend quickly with fingertips until the mixture resembles corn meal. The mixture should be cold to touch. Add the other pile of butter cubes. Use a pastry cutter or two knives and cut the butter into the flour until the fat is the size of peas. Sprinkle in enough of the water/lemon juice into flour and butter and stir lightly until a small amount of the dough holds together. Look for moist crumbs.

All flours absorb liquid differently. Only add as much water as you need to have lovely moist crumbs. Form the moist crumbs into two patties and wrap tightly with plastic wrap.

Refrigerate at least one hour, or up to three days. Dough can be frozen for several months.

To make flaky butter crust in a food processor, process flour and salt with the steel blade. Add half the butter and just flat-out process until the mixture looks like crumbs. Add the remaining butter and pulse briefly about 5 times to break up the butter. Start drizzling in the water with one hand while you do short little pulses with the other, about 10 little pulses. Only add as much water as you need! Proceed as above.

YIELD: TOP AND BOTTOM CRUSTS FOR ONE 9-INCH PIE

❖❖ EMMA CHASE CHERRY PIE

From Linda P. Thurston

½–¾ cup sugar	4 cups quality canned pitted
¼ cup flour	tart red cherries, drained
¼ teaspoon salt	2 tablespoons soft butter
1 cup cherry juice	One recipe Basic Flaky
	Butter Pie Crust

Preheat oven to 450°F.

In a medium saucepan, combine sugar, flour and salt. Stir in juice. Cook over low heat, stirring constantly until mixture is very thick. Add cherries and butter. If cherries are pale, add several drops of red food coloring.

Line a 9-inch glass pie plate with pastry. Flute edges creatively.

Pour slightly cooled cherry filling into the crust and top with a lattice crust.

Bake at 450°F for 10 minutes and reduce heat to 350°F and continue baking for about 45 minutes. If edges of crust start to brown, cover edges with foil.

YIELD: 1 SERVING

Cherry pie is a Kansas icon. Linda P. Thurston baked this pie and the one on the front cover. PHOTOGRAPH BY JANE P. MARSHALL

Steakholders of Kansas

Why did Kansas become a beef state? It's a matter of geography and transportation, of breathtaking Flint Hills pastureland and railroads.

The Texas cattle drives spawned the Kansas ranching industry. Kansas State University was a major caretaker of the industry.

Between 1866 and 1885, the trail boss and his wranglers drove millions of cattle from Texas to railheads in Kansas, first Abilene on the Chisholm Trail. Then Ellsworth, Wichita and finally Dodge City on the Great Western and the Goodnight Trails when the railroad got that far west. The trip took 25 to 100 days.

The 1871 drives herded an estimated 700,000 cattle to Kansas.

K-State agronomists also worked to keep meat on the tables of consumers whose numbers and income were growing. Their work focused on feed for livestock: Franklin A. Coffman helped make oats a successful crop in the United States; John. B. Sieglinger—the milo man—developed 23 commercial varieties of feed sorghum.

By 1885, the cattle business involved 1.3 million head of cattle, 28.2 million acres of pasture land, and an industry valued at $56.8 million. Today, the cattle industry is worth more than $6.24 billion to the state's economy.

Before she graduated in 2011 with a degree in animal sciences and industry, Kiley Stinson was active in Collegiate Cattlewomen and Collegiate Farm Bureau. She grew up in Lyon County. A member of Kansas Cattle Women, she offered these tips for grilling the perfect Kansas steak on a website called Kansas Beef Chat.

THE PERFECT KANSAS GRILLED STEAK

From Kiley Stinson

---

1 Kansas ribeye steak   **Salt**
Coarsely ground black pepper

Heat grill to hot. Season steak with salt and pepper. Place on hot grill.

When turning, pick up steak in one motion and place it back on the grill
with the same motion. Do not flip steak constantly or drag it over the grill.

Insert an instant-read thermometer horizontally into the side of the steak,
allow 10 to 15 seconds for the thermometer to register the internal temperature.
Cook steaks to 145°F for medium rare or 160°F for medium.

Total grilling time for a 1½-inch steak is 10 to 14 minutes for rare and 16 to
20 for medium.

Remove the steak from the heat and allow it to rest and relax at least five
minutes before cutting into it. This allows for the internal juices to redistribute
throughout the steak and the steak will relax and become tender.

YIELD: 1 SERVING

'Oh give me a home, where the buffalo roam...'

North American bison are roaming the Kansas prairie again.

K-State graduates Ed and Susan Dillinger own and operate the Lazy Heart D Bison Ranch, one of about 75 buffalo ranches representing more than 7,000 bison  in the state. She is an instructor in the College of Education. Their mission is to educate those who visit their ranch about the historic animals and "America's Original Red Meat." "We felt that kids were losing touch with agriculture," Susan Dillinger said. "We also wanted the farm to be a place where families, including our own, could come together."

Their herd of about 80 animals near Westmoreland entertains visitors from all over the world. Besides tours, the Dillingers sell buffalo meat, the darling of health-conscious red meat eaters. The taste has been described as "beef on steroids." It is low in fat and a good source of vitamin B12, iron, and omega-3 and omega-6 fatty acids.

Bison graze at the Lazy Heart D Bison Ranch near Westmoreland. Courtesy of Ed and Susan Dillinger

From cowboys (some with iPads, some without) to pie bakers, one in five Kansans work in jobs related to agriculture and food production. COURTESY OF DAVID MAYES, KANSAS STATE UNIVERSITY DIVISION OF COMMUNICATIONS AND MARKETING

LAZY HEART D RANCH BISON BRISKET ❖ ❖

From Susan and Ed Dillinger

4 cups (2 14.5-ounce cans) beef broth	¼ cup white vinegar
1 (10-ounce) bottle soy sauce	1 clove garlic, minced
¼ cup liquid smoke	1 bison brisket (any size) thawed or frozen

Mix broth, soy sauce, liquid smoke, vinegar and garlic. Place brisket in roasting pan and pour in marinade. Cover pan with foil and refrigerate for 24 hours, turning once.

Preheat oven to 300°F. Bake the brisket in marinade for 3 to 5 hours, depending on size. Internal temperature should be 155–160°F for medium.

Do not overcook. Meat should be fork tender, but not falling apart. Shred when hot or chill before slicing.

Yield: 2 to 3 servings per pound of bison

·5·
Cookbooks
—and—
Chemistry

Recipes

Food for Fifty: The Secret Ingredient

In 1982, Linda Thurston opened the Emma Chase Café in Cottonwood Falls, Kansas, armed with a doctorate in developmental and child psychology and a copy of *Food for Fifty*. The degree went in a drawer. The cookbook helped build the Emma Chase legend.

Thurston sold the café years ago and dusted off her doctorate. She is now associate dean and professor in the College of Education at Kansas State University. Her copy of *Food for Fifty* moved to Manhattan with her. Gravy stains and all. "I grew up in a large family and we always had hired hands at the table during harvest. I loved cooking for appreciative crowds. But at the Emma Chase, adapting favorite recipes for 35 for lunch or 100 for Sunday dinner wasn't an exercise in statistics. I needed guidance. I got it in *Food for Fifty*," Thurston explained. "It also helped me adapt recipes from the little Clementine Paddleford Book (*Cook Young Cookbook*, 1966)." (Full disclosure: Thurston is my twin sister.)

The book helped her figure out how to adapt recipes and gave her ideas for other foods. "The recipes were always delicious and reminiscent of home cooking. That was our specialty at the Emma Chase," she said. *Food for Fifty* has been a secret weapon…a secret ingredient…for professionals in quantity food production and food service management for more than 70 years.

In 1928, Mrs. Elma Stewart-Ibsen adapted the KSAC textbook *Practical Cookery* to quantity food-service cooking. Recipes from the college cafeteria were checked and rechecked. Each recipe made about 50 servings and, in most cases, did not appear in any other quality cookery recipe book. It was called *Feeding College Students on a Cooperative Basis*.

In 1937 the book was published in hardback and retitled *Food for Fifty* written by Bessie Brooks West and Sina Faye Fowler. Thurston's edition lists Grace Shugart, Mary Molt and Maxine Wilson as authors. Today the 880-page, 4.8-pound 13th edition is by Molt. She calls herself the "caretaker of the moment."

"The book keeps me connected to eating and recipe trends and keeps me better as a recipe developer," Dr. Molt said. "The book is a lot of fun. But it was a lot more fun when I was doing it with Grace."

Food for Fifty endures because, edition after edition, it offers valuable information such as serving sizes, weights and measures (1 pound tapioca after cooking, for example, yields 7½ cups) and menu terms. More importantly, cooks could trust the recipes. "It was developed in an academic setting," added Deb Canter, professor in hospitality management and dietetics. "As graduates took it with them into the world of work, it became the bible for institutional food service. If you go into a nursing home in the hinterlands, you will find a copy of *Food for Fifty*."

Online reviews second her statement: "I am a merchant seaman and have owned several editions of Food for 50. I have been using them for about 35 years on ship," wrote one fan.

"This is the third copy of this publication I've ordered in the past 12 years due to constant use…I call it my kitchen bible," wrote another.

A third admitted, "…never a week went by that I didn't consult it while running my bakery/deli in the Oregon Cascades. I must confess that I didn't tell customers my recipe source. I preferred they think me a genius or as having come from a family steeped in cooking history."

Kevin Roberts, associate professor and director of the restaurant management program, agrees. "At the restaurant I worked at in Iowa, we had a copy of *Food for Fifty*. We didn't use the recipes any longer; the restaurant had long since developed its own. But we used it as a reference for measures, weights and things like that."

"Quality and cost control—that's what those women were all about and that's the legacy they left us. *Food for Fifty* was the mother of standardized recipes in food production," Dr. Canter said. "K-State was such an early pacesetter in food service and dietetics."

Many students remember—and still use—this elegant, rich recipe. Make the chocolate ahead of time and make single portions. The recipe makes 16¾-cup servings. Serve with Lemon Ice Box Cookies or, for a chocolate overload, Sally's Touchdown Brownies. Grace Shugart loved cookies. The original *Food for Fifty* had 23 cookie recipes and variations for them.

GRACE SHUGART'S FRENCH CHOCOLATE ✤✤

Adapted from Food for Fifty

4.5 ounces unsweetened chocolate	Few grains of salt
¾ cup cold water	⅞ cup whipping cream
1 cup sugar	10 cups milk

Combine chocolate and water. Cook over direct heat, stirring constantly, for 5 minutes or until chocolate is melted. Remove from heat and beat with a wire whisk until smooth. (The 1937 edition called for using a rotary beater here.)

Add sugar and salt, return to heat and cook over hot water for 20 to 30 minutes or until thick. Chill.

Whip cream and fold into cold chocolate mixture. Heat milk to scalding. To serve, place 1 rounded tablespoon chocolate mixture in each serving cup. Fill cup with hot milk and stir until well blended. Serve immediately.

YIELD: 16 (¾ CUP) SERVINGS

Over the years, recipes have been dropped from the book and others added as new items became available on the market and food trends changed. Newer recipes are often ethnic and have bolder flavors.

"We took out recipes like Cheese Straws and Floating Islands and now you are seeing them on the Food Channel as the gourmet way to cook," author Mary Molt said. She also eliminated recipes that went out of style and may never be considered "gourmet." A few of the recipes left behind are Sweetbread Cutlets, Veal Soufflé, Braised Tongue, Jellied Chicken Loaf, Sweet Potato and Almond Croquettes, Hot Corn Sandwich and Pineapple-Pickle Salad.

❖❖ PINEAPPLE-PICKLE SALAD

From Food for Fifty *(1937)*

9 tablespoons plain gelatin	2 pounds pineapple, diced
1 pint vinegar	1 pound pickles, diced (the
3⅜ cups sugar	recipe does not indicate
1 tablespoon salt	type of pickle)
Few drops green food coloring	

Sprinkle gelatin over 1¼ quarts cold water and soak 10 minutes. Add 1½ quarts boiling water, vinegar, sugar, salt and food coloring. Stir until dissolved and chill. When mixture begins to set, add pineapple and pickles. Pour into molds or a flat 12 x 20-inch pan.

YIELD: 50 (OR MORE) SERVINGS

'They'll eat anything with gravy on it.'

An original drawing hung on the wall of the Emma Chase Café in Cottonwood Falls, a gift from the famous Etta Hulme, one of the few women editorial cartoonists in the country. The drawing shows a woman in an Emma Chase apron carrying a platter full of an upside down armadillo dripping with gravy. The text reads: "They'll eat anything with gravy on it."

Linda Thurston found this true of her Chase County customers, whose disdain for vegetables fit the he-man stereotype of farmers and ranchers. "I liked to fix unusual sides to go on the lunch plate specials," she said. "Of course, there was always a choice and most people chose green beans. But a few hardy souls would always try something like baked lima beans or beets with orange sauce."

Her fried chicken dinners with homemade rolls and freshly baked pies drew tourists from throughout the state. On Monday, she often served Chicken Tetrazzini using this recipe. Later editions of *Food for Fifty* call for more spaghetti, processed cheese and gravy made with water instead of milk.

✤✤ CHICKEN TETRAZZINI

From Food for Fifty *(7th edition)*

6 pounds (about 18 cups) cooked chicken, diced

6 ounces pimiento, chopped

2 tablespoons parsley, chopped

2½ pounds spaghetti, cooked according to package directions, tender but firm

1½ cups margarine or butter

1¼ cups finely chopped onion

1½ pounds mushrooms, sliced

1½ cups flour

1½ tablespoons salt

1 teaspoon pepper

2 quarts milk

1 quart chicken stock

1 pound cheddar cheese, shredded

Preheat oven to 350°F.

Combine chicken, pimiento and parsley. Set aside.

Sauté onion and mushrooms in butter. Blend in flour, salt and pepper. When flour bubbles, gradually add milk and chicken stock, stirring constantly. Cook until thickened.

Combine cooked spaghetti, chicken mixture and sauce. Pour into two greased 12 x 20 x 2-inch greased baking pans. Sprinkle half the cheese onto each pan. Bake for 35 to 40 minutes or until heated thoroughly and cheese is bubbly.

YIELD: 50 (8-OUNCE) PORTIONS

A Special Cookbook

A copy of *Practical Cookery* came in the mail a few months ago. It has a green hard cover and smells a little like a basement and was printed in 1962. Inside the textbook cover was written, in pencil, the names of two students: Ramona Starkey and Jane Pretzer. An attached note read: "I've had this for more than 40 years. It's your turn."

Ramona Starkey Kearns has been a dear friend since we shared secrets and textbooks in West Hall at K-State. I'd forgotten we shared *Practical Cookery*. And that she kept it. There is much modern practical advice in *Practical Cookery*: recipes for popcorn balls, bread pudding, broiled chicken, corn chowder, refrigerator rolls in 12 shapes and styles. But some have become antiquated: causes of defects in pickles, etiquette and service of afternoon tea, kidney casserole, lollypops, whipped non-fat dry milk solids, stuffed heart and Perfection Salad (yes, the one with gelatin, vinegar, celery and cabbage).

The 1910–11 KSAC catalog lists 15 food courses, including therapeutic cookery, dietetics and bread making. No textbook existed so the domestic science faculty created one from their collection of printed recipes in a loose-leaf form. The goal was to help students "conserve time spent in laboratory food preparation." The first edition was published in 1912 and it was revised 24 times before going out of print in 1975.

Martha S. Pittman, head of the Department of Foods Economics and Nutrition, wrote "The Story of the *Practical Cookery*" for *Home Economics News* in 1927: "Many a housewife has found this unpretentious little book invaluable in her home. It is a favorite gift for the bride.

"Even the spinster or bachelor finds occasional use of the book. In their case, it may be only a question of self-defense to determine what is wrong with food ordered in hope and consumed in disappointment, or it may be to indulge in an occasional orgy of cooking on their own part."

The book was filled with practical recipes for practical Kansas. Kansas homes and cooks were familiar with the book. Pittman commented that "in these 17 years many hundreds of young Kansas women have passed through the doors of the college via the foods laboratory route. Each has gone out into the world armed with a copy in the particular edition which happened to be in vogue at the time she was in college."

Its creators (none were listed in any edition but those first planners were Mary Pierce Van Zile, Ula M. Dow, Ida Rigney Migliario and Helen Huse

Collins) went for utility—no photos, no color, no folderol. People don't go for that kind of book any more. More people read cookbooks than cook from them. People open packages they buy at the supermarket and call it cooking. People eat a third of their meals outside the home. The average American spends more time watching food shows on television than actually cooking.

You can peruse the book today if you have a hankering for Cottage Cheese and Marmalade Sandwich, Spinach Timbales, Tongue Creole or Divinity. It is available online at http://archive.org/details/cu31924050717192. *Practical Cookery: A Compilation of Principles of Cookery and Recipes* by Kansas State University has been scanned from the Cornell University Library's print collections on an APT BookScan and converted to JPG 2000 format by Kirtas Technologies. The site for the scan from Harvard's collection is http://archive.org/details/practicalcooker00nutrgoog.

In 1950, about 15,000 copies, 12,000 outside of Kansas, were sold. The 24th and final edition of *Practical Cookery* was published by John Wiley in 1975. Royalties went into a scholarship fund for food and nutrition majors.

I don't remember how much we used *Practical Cookery* in Food Preparation and Meal Management class. Ramona doesn't either. But surely it should have more splatters than the tiny dot on "meats" page 117, some wrinkles in the vegetable section, yellowish swirls near Melba Toast, smudges between grapefruit sections and apple compote.

In forty years when it's her turn again, I'll ship the book back to Ramona. She won't cook from it. She probably won't read it. But she can hold it in her hands and remember our secrets and our lives in West and Justin. And grin.

The book includes recipes for 15 different flavors of ice cream. Many may remember this one from their youth. The flavor was a regional classic in New England and the Canadian Maritimes. Jamaicans think they invented it. C. W. Post developed the breakfast cereal in 1897 by running baked batter through a coffee grinder. He marketed it as a health food.

GRAPENUT ICE CREAM ✤ ✤

From Practical Cookery *(1962)*

1 cup Grapenuts	**1¼ teaspoons vanilla**
4 cups cream, thin	**1 pinch salt**
¾ cup sugar	

Soak Grapenuts in cream for 15 minutes. Add sugar, vanilla and salt. Mix thoroughly and freeze in ice cream maker following manufacturer's directions.

YIELD: 10 (½ CUP) SERVINGS

Floating Islands, little dabs of meringue "floating" in thin custard, is an old fashioned dish, originally French, that became trendy recently. Read this recipe from 1962, note the spellings and the garnishes. Cubes of jelly! Times have changed. Chefs today call it crème anglaise instead of plain vanilla custard. Wolfgang Puck spices his recipe for Floating Islands with rum and drizzles with almond-studded caramel sauce.

✧✧ FLOATING ISLANDS

From Practical Cookery *(1962)*

FOR SOFT CUSTARD:	FOR MERINGUES:
2 to 4 egg yolks	2 to 4 egg whites
¹⁄₁₆ teaspoon salt	⅛ teaspoon salt
2 tablespoons sugar	4 tablespoons sugar
1 cup milk	¼ teaspoon vanilla
¼ to ½ teaspoon flavoring	

Beat egg yolks with a fork just enough to mix as too much beating makes a frothy top. Add salt and sugar, and stir milk into the egg mixture.

Cook over hot, not boiling, water stirring constantly until foam disappears and mixture coats spoon. As soon as done, remove from hot water and set in cold water to stop cooking. Cool slightly and add flavoring. (No mention of what type of flavoring.) If custard curdles slightly, place in cold water and beat with a rotary egg beater.

To make meringues (the islands), beat egg whites with salt. Add sugar gradually during last half of beating. Continue beating until staff. Add vanilla.

Poach meringue by spoonful in hot water, turning once. Drain. Place meringue in serving dish and pour custard over it. Garnish with chopped nuts, "cocoanut," cherry, cubes of jelly or other desired material.

YIELD: 2 SERVINGS

Marjorie Honig Wonderlich graduated in family economics in 1971 with a diploma and a copy of *Practical Cookery*. Since then two of her standard recipes have been Beef Strognoff and Apple Crunch.

"And now they are mine," reports her daughter, Jessica Wonderlich. "My aunt (Janet Finney who works with the Department of Human Nutrition) and my mom made sure that my sisters and I all had our own copy of the *Practical Cookery* so we could carry a piece of our family's history with K-State with us. I love to experiment with new recipes and ingredients but I don't mess these two recipes."

BEEF STROGANOFF ✥ ✥

From Practical Cookery *(24th edition, 1975)*

1½ pounds top round steak, ½ inch thick	1 cup beef bouillon or beef broth
5 tablespoons flour	1 teaspoon lemon juice
3 tablespoons fat	½ teaspoon salt
1 medium onion, thinly sliced	¼ teaspoon pepper
1½ cups sliced fresh mushrooms	⅛ teaspoon dry mustard
	1 cup sour cream
	Hot noodles or rice

Cut meat in strips 1 by 2 inches long. Drench in 3 tablespoons flour and brown in fat. When brown, push meat to one side of pan, add onion. Cook until soft. Add mushrooms, ½ cup broth, lemon juice, salt, pepper and mustard to meat and onion mixture. Cover pan; cook over low heat for 45 to 60 minutes until meat is tender. Blend remaining 2 tablespoons flour with remaining broth, add to meat mixture. Cook over low heat until sauce is smooth and thickened, stirring constantly. Blend in sour cream and heat but do not boil.

Serve over hot noodles or rice.

YIELD: 6 SERVINGS

First Chemistry, then Cooking

Kansas State Agricultural College has offered instruction in chemistry since 1863. In the 1870s Benjamin F. Mudge taught agricultural chemistry. He had a national reputation as a geologist and taught all the natural sciences from meteorology to entomology.

Professor W. K. Kedzie led the plan to construct an $8,000 chemistry building whose lab was "second to none in the whole West," reported *The Industrialist*.

Kedzie taught chemistry to domestic science students in 1875, lecturing on "the chemistry of articles of food, such as butter and cheese, bread, tea and coffee; the chemistry of cooking, of ripening and preparation of fruits, dyeing and coloring bleaching, disinfectants and ventilation." Students had to take chemistry before they enrolled in food classes.

"Is not science as necessary in perfecting the art of making good bread as it is in raising good wheat?" wrote Sarah Josepha Hale, editor of *Godey's Lady's Book*, the leading women's magazine during the mid–19th century.

That attitude prevailed at K–State and was exemplified in the two legendary cookery books, *Practical Cookery* and *Food for Fifty*.

"To me, it's the idea that cooking is a science and it demands a formula. Before that it was what I call 'dump cooking,'" said Professor Deb Canter.

In 1922 KSAC awarded its first master of science degree in food economics and nutrition. In 1942 a PhD in food and nutrition was established.

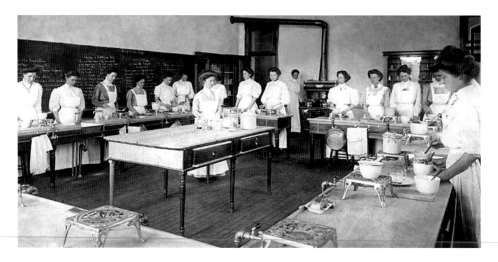

Young women, in class in Calvin Hall, had to pass chemistry before they could take cooking courses. Photo taken after 1908. Courtesy of Morse Department of Special Collections, Kansas State University Libraries

KITCHENETTE DOUGHNUTS ✥ ✥

From Practical Cookery *(1956)*

1 package (2 teaspoons) yeast	1 egg (use 2 for richer batter)
¼ cup water (105–110°F)	½ teaspoon vanilla
1 cup milk, lukewarm	½ cup shortening, melted
¼ cup sugar	Oil for frying
1 teaspoon salt	Sugar
3¼ cups flour, sifted	

For the basic beaten batter, soften yeast in water in a small bowl. Let stand 5 to 10 minutes. In a large bowl combine milk, ¼ cup sugar and salt. Add 2 cups flour then beat well. Add egg, softened yeast and vanilla. Beat well. Stir in shortening. Add more flour to make a stiff batter. Beat thoroughly until smooth.

Cover and let rise until bubbly, about 1 hour.

Drop batter by the teaspoonful into deep hot fat (350°F) and fry about 1½ minutes on each side or until light brown. Drain on paper towels.

Dredge hot doughnuts in sugar and serve.

YIELD: 3 DOZEN

A Different Kind of Laboratory

To many students the three limestone buildings in the wooded area across the road from Van Zile were mysterious places where students lived for nine weeks as part of their class requirements. They weren't dorms. They weren't apartments. They were more like boarding houses where the boarders ran the show and kept the books.

Between 1949 and the 1960s, Margaret Ahlborn Lodge, Ula Dow Cottage and Ellen H. Richards Lodge were live-in laboratories for home management students. Before they were built, space was rented in different houses in Manhattan for coeds to learn "valuable lessons that pertained to standards of living and standards of food." In the home management houses, they practiced what they learned in the classroom about household management to prepare them to run their own homes and to prepare them to be teachers and extension agents.

Times changed; coursework changed; enrollment changed. By 1983, the "practice houses" were reassigned for other uses. Today the buildings have been renovated and joined as the Campus Creek Complex, housing research, education and service for the Family Center and the Speech and Hearing Center.

Mary Jeanne Scoby Jensen—whose family tree is so purple that her Scoby grandparents now have 60 family members and spouses who attended K-State— lived there during the fall of 1962. She sent a packet of recipes she and her housemates cooked that fall, "the result of a delightful 9 weeks of good eating, fun experiences and new friends," she said. The pages included this note: "Those cooking experts contributing to this masterpiece were Judy Holle, Mary Jo Charvat, Mary Jeanne Scoby, Helen Wegman, Kathy Otljen, Louis Evans, Pat (the diplomat) Mollhagen and me, Bev (the married lady) Dunning."

Although the recipes Mrs. Jensen recommended are quick ones, the group also used recipes for Chicken Kiev and Spumone with eggnog, pistachio, chocolate and raspberry layers. One does raise an eyebrow at the Cherries Jubilee recipe that calls for ½ cup of brandy.

Mrs. Jensen says her children loved these when they were growing up.

PIZZA SANDWICHES ✤✤

Home Management House (1962)

---

12 ounces sausages (such as Brown 'N Serve)	1½ cups shredded cheddar cheese (about 6 ounces)
8 English muffins, split	3 teaspoons dried oregano
8 ounces tomato paste	

Cut each sausage into 8 crosswise slices. Spread muffin halves with tomato paste then sprinkle with cheese and oregano. Top with sausage slices.

Place muffins on cookie sheet and toast under broiler until bubbly. Serve immediately.

YIELD: 16 PIZZAS. ALLOW AT LEAST TWO PER PERSON.

From the Classroom to the Dining Room

Betsy Barrett tells the story of the stricken student, the K–State Union elevator and a hog's head. Professor Barrett's students were working on a food production dinner (and a grade!) in the 1990s. When the time for the grand entrance neared, a student hefted the platter with the roasted, decorated hog and stepped into the elevator. As the elevator rose to the second-floor dining room, Dr. Barrett heard a loud "plop." The door opened to reveal students with horrified looks on their faces and a hog's head on the floor.

They put the head back on the platter, arranged the flowers back around the head and marched into the banquet hall. "Nobody ever knew the difference," Dr. Barrett laughed. She refused to name the students involved.

Food productions aren't often so dramatic. But they continue to be a cooperative effort between the hospitality management and dietetics (formerly institutional economics) department and the university dining services.

Before Betty Allen graduated in 1957 and became a home economics teacher, she took a school food service course. "We were required to work in the Manhattan school lunch rooms and also serve banquets," she recalls. "I remember the banquets served on campus had a favorite dessert of pumpkin tarts. I've been serving them for more than 50 years."

The pecan layer makes them special. Mix 2 tablespoons melted butter, ¼ cup brown sugar and ¼ cup chopped pecans. Spread on the bottom of unbaked pie or tart shells, fill with a favorite pumpkin pie recipe and bake according to the pie instructions.

Today the semester's finale for HMD 342 Food Production classes is in the Gold Room of Derby Dining Center. This spring tickets cost $15. Students presented Floridian, Cajun/Creole and midwestern cuisines. The midwestern menu included Rosemary Roasted Pork Loin with Mushroom Sauce, Oatmeal Rolls and Kansas Dirt.

Students have researched, planned and prepared menus from cultures around the world, say Professors Missy Schrader and Sheryl Klobasa. This recipe, part of a Sicilian meal students prepared in 2005, is a favorite.

Students learned to candle eggs at an off-campus egg business, Perry Packing Company, in Manhattan, 1939. Courtesy of Morse Department of Special Collections, Kansas State University Libraries

ARANCINI (SICILIAN RICE BALLS) ✠✠ WITH MARINARA

From HMD 342 Student Final Project Dinners

2 cups uncooked Italian Aborio or American Carolina rice

1 cup grated Romano cheese

1 (10-ounce) package frozen green peas, thawed

2 eggs

1 pound Provolone cheese in ½ inch cubes

1 cup flour

1 cup cold water

2 cups dried bread crumbs

3 cups canola oil for deep frying

2 cups marinara sauce, heated

Boil the rice in salted water until tender as directed on package. Drain. Cool rice to 100–115°F and then add Romano cheese, peas and eggs and mix well. Cool completely to 40°F.

To form Arancini, take ⅓ to ½ cup of rice mixture and form a ball. Push one cube of provolone into the middle of the rice ball and reshape into a uniform ball. Complete until all the rice mixture is formed.

Mix flour with water to form a paste. Coat each rice ball in paste and then roll in bread crumbs until completely coated. Refrigerate at least 1 hour or overnight.

Preheat oven to 450°F.

When ready to fry Arancini, heat the oil to 375°F in a deep fat fryer or large cast iron pot. Fry until golden brown and finish in a 450°F oven until the internal temperature reaches 165°F (about 15 minutes).

Serve hot with marinara sauce.

Yield: 14 to 16 rice balls

'I never saw a purple pie...until now'

Nutrition scientists at K-State traded test tubes for pie tins in 2010 to raise funds to support student travel and research. At Thanksgiving PhD candidate Soyoung Lim and master's degree student Tzu-Yu Chen baked and sold 40 Purple Pride Sweet Potato Pies.

The story begins with a sweet potato breeder named Ted Carey, a horticulture professor before he moved to Ghana to work with the International Potato Center. At K-State, Carey got seeds from purple sweet potato parent plants from the potato center's germplasma bank in Peru. He stuck the seeds in fertile Kansas soil. When they grew, he cloned the most colorful ones.

Enter George Wang, research scientist in the Department of Human Nutrition. The bright purple color meant the potatoes were loaded with anthocyanin, a pigment associated with reduced risk of cancer. Cancer preventative nutrition is Wang's specialty. Did the potatoes have anti-cancer abilities? He believes so. "The pies could be used to test bioavailablity of anthocyanins in humans," he said.

The food research path illustrates the progress of a discipline molded by scientific and cultural advancement. In 1893 research projects (then called experiments) were in canning fruits and qualities of pork roasts from animals fed wheat, corn or "ordinary ration." Then came studies in eating soybeans and alfalfa biscuits and the digestibility of beef cooked at two temperatures. In the early 1920s, professors and students conducted experiments with vitamins A and C, waste in food preparation, vitamin B content in breads from wheat products, diets of overweight adolescents and calcium retention in adolescent girls. In the late 20th century, themes included consumer aspects of such products such as acceptability of frozen chocolate pies, nutrition education, nutrition labeling and effects of a running lifestyle.

Although the K-State potatoes are not on the market yet, any purple-colored version will work with the recipe.

PURPLE PRIDE SWEET POTATO PIE ✧✧

1 (1-pound) purple sweet potato	2 eggs
½ cup butter, softened	½ teaspoon ground nutmeg
½ cup sugar	½ teaspoon ground cinnamon
½ cup brown sugar	1 teaspoon vanilla
½ cup milk	1 (9-inch) unbaked pie crust

Preheat oven to 350°F.

Boil sweet potato whole in skin for 40 to 50 minutes or until done. Run cold water over the sweet potato and remove the skin. Mash potato in a food processor until smooth. Add butter, sugars, milk, eggs, nutmeg, cinnamon and vanilla. Pulse until the mixture is smooth. Turn out into prepared pie pastry.

Bake for 55 to 60 minutes or until knife inserted in center comes out clean.

YIELD: 6 TO 8 SERVINGS

·6·
Chefs, Cooks
—— *and* ——
Road Trips

Recipes

Family Tradition: Cherry Pie and Brownies

The morning of her wedding on June 12, 1918, Esther Ericson made a cherry pie.

Almost every June 12 after that, Esther Ericson Wreath baked a cherry pie. "During the Depression and Dust Bowl years, if the cherry trees did not produce, there was no pie," recalled her daughter, Martha Wreath Streeter, in a book she published in 1996 for her family called *More Than I Expected*.

George Wreath and Esther Ericson courted for 9 years before they married and moved into a house at 1030 Houston Street. He was born in 1883 south of Olsburg and, despite only a 6th-grade education, was hog herdsman at KSAC and an extension livestock specialist in the early 1900s. His expertise was Duroc hogs.

His pie-baking bride was born in 1879. Her father was a Swedish immigrant who homesteaded in the Lower Seven Mile community in Riley County. Esther Ericson Wreath, who studied at Kansas State Agricultural College and taught in the community for 18 years, was famous for her "feather rolls."

Ladies Day dress and duster, ca. 1910. COURTESY OF DAVID MAYES, KANSAS STATE UNIVERSITY DIVISION OF COMMUNICATIONS AND MARKETING, K-STATE HISTORIC COSTUME AND TEXTILE MUSEUM, 1985.16.23AB. GIFT OF NANCY VEAL GALLOWAY.

"Mother had made the yeast dough the morning before, then punched it down and shaped it into large flat rolls. She threw a clean tea towel over them and set them on a chair behind the big wood stove in the living room. By morning they were light as a feather," Mrs. Streeter wrote.

The rolls were served with butter and cherry preserves, fruit complements of the pie-cherry trees.

On many Sundays, the family made candy—butterscotch, chocolate fudge, penuche, divinity or taffy. Box and pie suppers added spice to high school activities in the 1930s. At these money-raising events, each young woman prepared and boxed a meal for two. Each box was auctioned off and the highest bidder got supper and a date for the evening. Boxes of the especially popular girls brought $1, Mrs. Streeter wrote. Most sold for around 35 cents.

Martha Wreath Streeter married into another family with strong food—and K-State—traditions. Charles Streeter grew up on a farm near Milford. His mother, Catherine Hutchinson Streeter, graduated in 1907 in home economics from K-State and, during the Depression, sold homemade cottage cheese. "She was a very good cook who made a freezer of ice cream every Sunday," her son remembered.

Charles Streeter earned bachelor's and master's degrees in agricultural economics at K-State where he was a researcher. In the early 1960s he became concessionaire at City Park and CiCo park and moved on to start the Vista Restaurant chain.

The first Vista Hamburger Drive-In, opened in June 1964, was a Manhattan novelty, Mrs. Streeter recalled. "It allowed persons to order and pick up dinner without leaving their cars." It featured an ICEE machine, a 1958 invention of Mr. Streeter's cousin, Omar Knedlik, who owned a Dairy Queen in Coffeeville.

Mr. Streeter, who died in 1984, was chosen for the Kansas Restaurant Association Hall of Fame in 1982. Mrs. Streeter was president of the Kansas 4-H Foundation Board of Trustees, on the board of the alumni association and the K-State Foundation. She received the Distinguished Service Award in Human Ecology in 1991 and in 1988 was named Kansas Home Economist of the Year.

Floodwaters in 1951 rise on the 200 block of Poyntz. Seven feet of water stood in the Wareham Hotel. Note the café signs. COURTESY OF THE RILEY COUNTY HISTORICAL SOCIETY

The drive-in became an instant hangout for students, attracted by its prices. On game days, Wildcat fans and alumni still gather at the Vista, which moved to the hillside on Tuttle Creek Boulevard after the 1951 flood, for milkshakes and chili, made from the same recipe Charles and Martha used beginning in 1941.

Brownies are baked from the same recipe Martha Streeter taught her home economics students at Wamego High School 46 years ago. They are the foundation for the Vista's famous Hot Fudge Brownie dessert. Many a student who frequented the early days of the Vista still swoons over that fudge sauce.

Like Charles Streeter before them, current owners Brad and Karen Streeter were elected to the Kansas Restaurant Association Hall of Fame in 2007. Brad Streeter says the brownie recipe won many purple ribbons at the state fair.

But he won't give it up.

This recipe from Martha Streeter is not served at the drive-in but was a favorite of hers.

STRAWBERRY SPINACH SALAD ✤ ✤

From Martha Streeter

Published in Essence of Kansas: 4-H Cookbook, Taste Two *(1994)*

½ **cup sugar**

2 **tablespoons sesame seeds**

1 **tablespoon poppy seeds**

1½ **teaspoons minced onion**

¼ **teaspoon Worcestershire sauce**

¼ **teaspoon pepper**

½ **cup salad oil**

¼ **cup cider vinegar**

1 **bunch fresh spinach**

1 **pint fresh strawberries, hulled**
   and cut in half

In a blender, process sugar, sesame seeds, poppy seeds, onion, Worcestershire sauce and pepper for 1 minute. Add oil and vinegar and continue to process until blended.

Assemble spinach and strawberries in a large glass salad bowl and chill until serving time. Pour dressing over salad and toss.

YIELD: 6 SERVINGS

'We ate a lot of meatloaf.'

In 1951 nearly 5,000 students attended K-State. One of them was Warren Prawl. Most male students had to fend for themselves at mealtime, he reminisced. Coeds lived in Putnam, Boyd or Van Zile and ate in dining halls there. But there were no dormitories for male students and they huddled in basements and rooming houses sprinkled on the streets near campus.

One year "there were six of us in a basement in a private home," he recalled, noting that two had cars. "I boarded across the street from the Glenn Beck Dairy Barn (then called the Old Dairy Barn) and worked there for three years. There were four boys, taking either the morning shift or the evening shift to milk cows. During vacations I would eat there. We had cheese, crackers and milk."

Mr. Prawl ate at The Chef downtown because it was cheapest—75 cents a meal. He usually ordered breaded steak. Pie cost an extra 15 cents.

Other culinary choices were Sheu's Café downtown and at the Mar Café in Aggieville next to Palace Drug. Students lined up for chocolate dip cones at Norma and Jackson Todd's Dairy Queen in Aggieville. It opened in 1953 or '54 and was the first Dairy Queen in town.

A view of the 200 and 300 blocks of Poyntz Avenue in Manhattan, ca. 1953. Note the number of dining establishments. COURTESY OF THE RILEY COUNTY HISTORICAL SOCIETY

Before Harry's there was the Wareham Hotel Dining Room in the Wareham Hotel. Built by Harry Pratt Wareham in 1925, it was the city's first "skyscraper" and included dining rooms, a coffee room, hotel rooms and apartments. The top floor was Mr. Wareham's private residence. COURTESY OF THE RILEY COUNTY HISTORICAL SOCIETY

Dining halls and most restaurants closed on Sunday nights, leaving students to heat canned spaghetti in their rooms or forage from friends with kitchens. Many headed to the Wesley Foundation which served a church service and dinner, made by students.

On other days, Prawl dined at the dairy bar, then in West Waters where the creamery was. He also recalled the old Student Union, fashioned from World War II barracks on the site of the present union, where he ate sandwiches and other quick order items.

"We ate a lot of meatloaf," said Prawl, Class of '54 and retired from the College of Education and Extension. "It was cheap."

Marge Davidson remembers the legendary hamburgers at The Chef. A fancy meal meant visiting the Gillette Hotel on 4th and Houston. The dining room walls were covered with imported paper and the tables were draped in white and topped with finger bowls. On one visit, young Miss Marge drank from one. "It embarrassed my mother to tears. She was a white glove lady," she recalled.

Today students have never seen a finger bowl and have witnessed white gloves only in old movies. They eat hamburgers, tacos and burritos, spicy beef with snow peas. When Mom and Dad pick up the check, they order steak. Or, if at Harry's on Poyntz, they order the meatloaf dinner, an elegant tower of meat and garlic smashed potatoes with a Cabernet demi-glace and sautéed asparagus. Owners Evan and Andrea Grier are graduates of K-State's hospitality management program.

❖❖ HARRY'S FAMOUS MEATLOAF

From Evan Grier

2 large carrots
1 cup fresh parsley
1 teaspoon fresh rosemary
4 cloves garlic
2 stalks celery, diced
1 yellow onion, cut into chunks
1 cup ketchup
4 teaspoons mustard powder
4 teaspoons kosher salt
2 teaspoons coarse ground
    black pepper
2 teaspoons Sriracha
    (Thai hot sauce)
4 eggs, beaten
½ loaf white bread, crusts
    removed (8 slices or
    about 8 ounces)
1 pound ground beef
1 pound ground veal
    (or turkey breast)
1 pound ground pork

Preheat oven to 350°F.

In a food processer, pulse carrots, parsley, rosemary and garlic until finely chopped. Transfer to a large bowl.

To processer bowl add celery and onion. Pulse until finely chopped. Add to carrot mixture. Add ketchup, mustard, salt, pepper, Sriracha and eggs. Mix thoroughly.

With the processor, pulse bread into crumbs, about 2½ cups. Add crumbs and meat to carrot mixture. Mix thoroughly.

Press into 2 loaf or other baking pans as desired. Cover each loaf with topping. Bake for 1 hour or until done.

TOPPING:

2 tablespoons canola oil
1 medium onion, finely
    chopped
1 cup ketchup
¼ cup brown sugar
2 tablespoons dry mustard

Heat oil in a skillet; sauté onion until lightly browned. Add ketchup, brown sugar and mustard. Stir to thoroughly combine.

YIELD: 12 SERVINGS

The Chef

The Chef reincarnated opened in 2008 at 111 South 4th Street, the site of the original Chef that closed in 1986. The Riley County Historical Society offered owners Kurstin Harris, Kevin Harris and Zach Filbert the original neon sign.

One of the "coffee boys" is Bob Limbocker who owned The Chef in the 1980s. His father, Charles "Cotton" Limbocker, opened the original café in 1943. From the horseshoe counter, he plated pies-and-meatloaf home cooking. Bob and Teryl Limbocker took over and expanded the menu and the space.

On a weekend you will probably have to wait for a table. But the staff makes sure you have a cup of The Chef Blend coffee in hand. It's roasted and blended at nearby Radina's Coffeehouse & Roastery. The top breakfast orders are classic breakfast, breakfast burrito (with chorizo gravy) and biscuits and gravy.

Manhattan's Coffeehouse

While he was pursuing a political science degree at K-State in the late 1980s, Wade Radina worked as a barista at 2-year-old Espresso Royale Caffe in Aggieville. He continued to work for the company during the '90s then moved to Colorado where he got an MBA.

In 2001 the College of Business Administration offered Radina a position teaching operations management and the family moved back to Manhattan. Wade and Annette bought the coffeehouse and renamed it Radina's Coffeehouse & Roastery. He believes it may be one of the oldest continuously operating coffeehouses in Kansas, if not the Midwest.

Radina's reasoning was grounded in philosophy as well as business. "We need to live in a community with a great coffeehouse. I have a deep passion for coffeehouses and coffee. Coffeehouses serve a vital community function," he said.

Radina's roasts coffee every other day for his three locations and employees include three full-time and three part-time bakers who make all the pastries from scratch. The café also serves soup, sandwiches and gelato. They use locally produced Jersey milk and about 300 pounds of Kansas grown and milled flour.

Since 2001 Radina's has sold about 40,000 servings of this custard, adapted from a family recipe from Radina's grandmother who emigrated from Czechoslovakia.

❖❖ GRANDMA'S CUSTARD

From Wade Radina

24 eggs	1 teaspoon salt
4 cups sugar	16 cups light cream such
1 tablespoon vanilla	as half and half

Preheat oven to 325°F.

Whisk together eggs, sugar, vanilla and salt. Heat cream to scalding, just below boiling.

Very slowly, while beating the egg mixture, add cream. Strain into custard cups.

Set cups in large baking pan of hot water ¾ inches deep, place pan in oven and bake for 50–55 minutes or until knife inserted near center comes out clean (160°F in the center).

Chill before serving.

YIELD: 32 SERVINGS

Going Gourmet in the Heartland

Scott Benjamin, chef and owner of 4 Olives Restaurant and Wine Bar in Manhattan, may serve American Bison Osso Buco on a bed of roasted wild mushroom risotto paired with Justin Cabernet Sauvignon one week and Pan-seared Idaho Trout with Almonds finished with mixed sweet peppers sautéed in tomato vinaigrette paired with Lioco Sonoma Chardonnay the next.

For Sunday brunch he serves Duroc pork rib chops and eggs. The pork comes from Amy and Craig Good's farm in Olsburg. Mr. Good is a K-State graduate.

4 Olives, which opened in 2004, became the first Kansas restaurant to be nominated for the James Beard Foundation for Outstanding Wine Program and has received the Wine Spectator Award for Excellence every year since 2005. It is one of only 700 restaurants in the world to be honored with a Wine Spectator Best of Award of Excellence.

Rachel Benjamin, 4 Olives pastry chef, creates Mascarpone Cheesecake, Grasshopper Torte, Chocolate Carmel Pots de Crème with Homemade Toffee and other culinary delights. The chefs, both K-Staters, pride themselves in using locally grown products as much as they can.

"We get a ton of morels around here in the spring, so many in fact that I dry many pounds of them each year and then use them in sauces throughout the year. Here is one of my favorite ways to use them in the winter," Scott said. This is a four-step process: the rub, the morel sauce, the bread rings and the steaks.

SCOTT BENJAMIN'S MORELS
AND LOST BREAD FILET MIGNON
From Scott Benjamon for 4 Olives

4 (6–8 ounce) filet mignon
    steaks

RUB:

4 cloves roasted garlic

1 tablespoon chopped fresh
    thyme

2 tablespoons chopped fresh
    parsley

1 teaspoon chopped fresh
    rosemary

2 teaspoons black peppercorns

2 teaspoons coarse sea salt

½ cup olive oil

Combine rub ingredients in blender; blend until peppercorns are ground and rub has an even texture.

SAUCE:

4 ounces dried morels

4 cups hot water

2 tablespoons butter

¼ cup minced shallots

1 cup Spanish cream sherry

3 cups heavy cream

Salt and black pepper to taste

Soak morels for one hour in water. Remove with slotted spoon, strain the water and cook to reduce to 1 cup. Set aside.

In small saucepan, cook shallots in butter until they are slightly soft. Add the rehydrated morels and cream sherry. Cook until reduced by half. Add cream and reduced morel-water stock and cook until thick. Season with salt and black pepper.

LOST BREAD RINGS:

2-inch thick slices artisan
  whole wheat bread

4 eggs

1 cup cream

½ cup milk

½ teaspoon salt

2 tablespoons honey

Pinch of five spice powder

Use an 18.6-ounce soup can or rocks glass to punch out 4–6 rings of 2-inch thick slices of wheat bread. Let the bread dry overnight.

Combine eggs, cream, milk, salt, honey and spice in a bowl and set aside.

Preheat oven to 425°F. About 30 minutes before grilling, coat steaks with the rub and let rest in the refrigerator.

Bring to room temperature and grill on hot grill for a few minutes on each side. Finish to medium rare (internal temperature of 125°F) in a 425°F oven. Let rest before serving. Note that after the steaks come out of the oven, they will continue to cook, probably 5 to 10 degrees more. Please don't overcook steaks.

While steaks are cooking, soak dried bread circles in egg/cream mixture for 1 to 2 minutes, then pan fry on griddle or sauté pan in a little butter, and finish in the 425°F oven until firm again.

Place filet on top of "French toast" and top with a few morels and a ladle of sauce. Some nice sides are spiced carrots, grilled zucchini or grilled asparagus.

Yield: 4 servings

Living with History

History professors Jim Sherow and Bonnie Lynn-Sherow are known for their expertise in regional history and their community activism. But to those who visit their bed and breakfast, Daughters House Inn on 617 Colorado Street, they are famous for their breakfast sandwiches.

The inn was designed by Herbert McCure Hadley, the first licensed architect in Kansas, and built in 1892 from native limestone and cedar shakes. It is on the National Register of Historic Places.

Lynn-Sherow says the key to the breakfast sandwich is high quality ingredients...and Wildcat Breakfast Sausage from K-State's Call Hall. If you don't keep hens for fresh eggs, look for local eggs. She garnishes the sandwich with hot sauce, salsa, sliced avocado or finely chopped tomato with olive.

Earl Fitzgerald and Will Gore, who owned a bakery in Manhattan with his sister Maggie around 1920, take a break. Note the loaves of bread stored vertically on the rack. COURTESY OF THE RILEY COUNTY HISTORICAL SOCIETY

DAUGHTERS HOUSE BREAKFAST SANDWICHES ✤✤

From Bonnie Lynn-Sherow

½ pound ground **Wildcat Breakfast Sausage**, thawed
Fresh garden herbs (a combination of basil, fresh oregano, parsley or cilantro)
⅛ teaspoon olive oil

4 high quality whole wheat **English muffins**
4 **giant-sized eggs** from our backyard hens
4 ⅛-inch thick slices Vermont aged cheddar cheese
Seasoning

Divide the sausage into four pieces. Lightly press each piece into a patty just a little larger than the muffin in diameter. Cook on a hot griddle, one or two minutes a side, pressing down on the patty, squeezing out excess fat at the end of cooking. Drain on a paper towel and place in a warming drawer or near a heat source to stay warm. Season to taste with fresh ground pepper and salt or a Cajun or other commercial seasoning.

Lightly chop the herbs, mix with a scant ⅛ teaspoon of olive oil, salt and pepper.

Lightly coat a four-egg poaching pan with non-stick spray. Fill a shallow pan with 1 inch of water and bring to a boil. Crack each egg into a saucer and then carefully transfer to the poaching pan. Lower pan into water (water should NOT cover eggs!) and cook for about three minutes. Place a lid over the pan for the last minute.

Lightly toast the English muffins in a toaster, or lightly brush with olive oil or other vegetable oil and place on a cookie sheet in the oven under "broil" for no longer than a minute or two.

On four heat-proof plates, place the bottom halves of the muffin, then a sausage patty, followed by a poached egg and the cheddar cheese. Place the plates under the broiler for just a half minute or until the cheddar begins to droop. It also works to put the plates, one at a time, in the microwave for about 45 seconds on HIGH.

Mound the herb mixture on top of the cheese. Cover with the other half of the muffins and serve immediately.

YIELD: 4 SANDWICHES

Road Trips

Before Anthony Bourdain, Guy Fieri and Jane and Michael Stern, there was *The Ford Treasury of Favorite Recipes from Famous Eating Places.*

Highways improved. The automobile became more reliable and comfortable. The Ford Motor Company published the little booklets in the 1940s and '50s to encourage Americans to hit the road.

But before President Eisenhower birthed the interstate system and roads resembled airport runways whose purpose was getting from here to there as fast as possible, before that mentality ushered in fast food havoc, before fast cars and rising speed limits allowed drivers to barrel through the landscape, a road trip meant meandering through small towns and stopping at local eateries. By the 1920s, K-State students could rent an open Ford for 12 cents a mile with no time charge until after 6 p.m.

"The Ford Times," delivered free to all Ford

In 1946 Frank M. Crooke opened Crooke's Rexall Drugs at the southeast corner of Poyntz and South Fourth Street in what was called the Ulrich block of Manhattan. It included a fancy soda fountain. The building had been used as a drugstore since it was built by the Ulrich family in 1893. College dances were reportedly held in 1895 in the Ulrich building. COURTESY OF THE RILEY COUNTY HISTORICAL SOCIETY

buyers starting in 1908, was compiled into three cookbooks that sold nearly half a million copies and encouraged destination dining. The three featured stops in Kansas were the Brookville Hotel in the old cattle town of Brookville, Cohen's Chicken House near Junction City and the Swedish Diner south of Salina.

The original Brookville Hotel dates to the 1870s. The famous family-style chicken dinners were instituted in 1915, a special treat for the K-State community who drove over to fill up on an old-fashioned Kansas chicken dinner. In 2000 the restaurant moved to Abilene off I-70. The Sterns, by the way, call it "legendary, worth driving from anyplace."

This is the only recipe in the entire *Teatime to Tailgates* book that uses raw eggs. According to the Federal Drug Administration, you may substitute pasteurized eggs or egg products, available at grocery stores, for raw eggs in a recipe.

BROOKVILLE HOTEL'S OLD-FASHIONED ICE CREAM ❖ ❖

Published in The Ford Treasury of Favorite Recipes from Famous Eating Places

4 eggs	3 cups heavy cream
2 cups sugar	1 tablespoon vanilla
½ teaspoon salt	2 quarts whole milk

Beat eggs until very light. Gradually add sugar and salt. Beat mixture well. Then add cream and vanilla. Add milk last. Allow about 2½ inches of swelling in the freezer can. Freeze in dasher type old-fashioned ice-cream freezer.

YIELD: 1 GALLON

BROOKVILLE HOTEL'S SWEET AND SOUR COLESLAW ❖ ❖

From the Brookville Hotel

1½ pounds green cabbage, shredded, well chilled	⅔ cup sugar
	⅓ cup cider vinegar
1 teaspoon salt	1 cup whipping cream

To thoroughly chilled cabbage, mix salt, sugar, vinegar and cream. Chill and serve.

YIELD: 8 SERVINGS

The day Cohen's Chicken House burned down was a mournful day for fried chicken lovers at K-State. Fort Riley brought Sam Cohen to Kansas during World War I. He stayed to serve his specialty—Chicken on a Tray—and get a coveted listing in the mobile guide. Calvin Trillin wrote about Cohen's in *The New Yorker* in 1975.

✥✥ COHEN'S CHICKEN HOUSE ORANGE ROLLS

Published in The Ford Treasury of Favorite Recipes from Famous Eating Places

¾ cup sugar	7–8 cups flour (enough for a
1 teaspoon salt	soft dough)
2 eggs	
1 cup lukewarm milk	ORANGE MIXTURE:
1 cup warm water	½ cup butter
1 cake yeast, or substitute 1	1 cup sugar
(2¼ teaspoons) package	Grated rind (zest) from
active dry yeast	2 oranges

Melt orange mixture ingredients together in a skillet until mixture thickens slightly. Set aside.

Cream sugar, salt and eggs. Add milk and yeast that has been dissolved in the warm water. Add flour a little at a time, stirring until dough does not stick to greased hands. Place in a large greased bowl, cover with plastic wrap and set aside to rise for 30 minutes.

Preheat oven to 350°F.

Spread with part of the orange mixture. Roll up dough lengthwise and cut into 1½-inch squares. Prepare the remaining dough the same way. Place rolls on a baking sheet, cover loosely with a clean towel, and set aside to rise for 20 minutes. Bake for 20 minutes, or until light golden brown and rolls sound hollow when tapped on the bottoms.

YIELD: 3 DOZEN

Fred Harvey recruited young women from the East to work in his restaurants along the Santa Fe rail line that stretched across Kansas. They were called Harvey Girls, never waitresses.

For 150 years, K-Staters have loved donuts. In the 1980s, they ate "Yum-Yums," a special type of fried Danish roll created at Swannie's in the alley of 225 Poyntz. Richard "Swannie" Swanson fried his last batch of donuts on December 12, 1985. Courtesy of the Riley County Historical Society and the Manhattan Mercury

Fred Harvey, His Girls and White Table Cloths

The Harvey Houses and dining cars were the epitome of elegant cuisine and service in the late 19th century.

Fred Harvey has been credited with bringing white tablecloth service, quality restaurant food and pretty girls to Kansas and the southwest. At one time he had 75 Harvey Houses along the 12,000-mile Santa Fe line. No doubt hundreds of K-State students, faculty and visitors ate at one or more Harvey Houses in Kansas.

Harvey, a British-born businessman from Leavenworth, opened his first Harvey House in Topeka on November 4, 1876. It had a U-shaped lunchroom counter and a dining room.

Meals cost 35 cents. A typical breakfast was steak and eggs, 6 pan-sized wheat cakes with maple syrup, hashed brown potatoes, and apple pie and coffee for dessert. It closed in 1940.

Harvey brought young women from the east to work in his restaurants. Ages 18 to 30, "of good character, attractive and intelligent," they lived in dorms under the watchful eyes of matrons. They wore black and white uniforms and had to promise not to marry for a year. Some estimate that 100,000 Harvey Girls—they were never called waitresses—came west to work.

In 1878 Harvey operated the Clifton House in Florence, Kansas. He hired seven Harvey Girls. The house served meals to three trains daily, each train carrying about 50 diners. Each passenger paid 75 cents for dinner. The crew ate for 25 cents. It closed in 1900 and the building is now a museum.

He moved passenger service headquarters to Newton in 1900 (after the rowdy cowboys left) and by 1921 the laundry there cleaned 4 million pieces a year. In 1930 he built a new Newton Harvey Hotel that was a replica of Shakespeare's home in England.

When cattle shipping yards moved to Dodge City, Harvey installed a lunchroom in a boxcar on stilts near the tracks in 1896. "The architecture was crude, the town even cruder, but Fred Harvey's food and service was [sic] not," one historian wrote.

When Fred Harvey died in 1901 at age 65, he had 20 dining cars and 45 eateries in 12 states. He is credited with creating the first restaurant chain in the nation.

These recipes demonstrate the sophistication and appeal of Harvey's menus. Erich Walther was in charge of the Santa Fe Dining Car Commissary in Chicago where meats were cut and prepared "oven-ready" before being taken aboard the dining car kitchens. Commissaries were also located in Kansas City, Houston, Clovis, Bakersfield and Los Angeles.

ROULADE OF BEEF ✤ ✤

By Erich Walther
Fred Harvey Santa-Fe Dining Car Service

4 (8-ounce) pieces sirloin steak	1 large dill pickle, cut lengthwise into fourths
2 teaspoons salt	¼ cup flour
¼ teaspoon pepper	4 teaspoons butter
4 slices bacon	2 cups beef broth
2 thick slices onion, cut in half	2 tablespoons catsup

Flatten steaks with a meat cleaver until very thin; season with salt and pepper. On each steak, place a slice of bacon, ½ onion slice and one pickle stick. Roll up steak and tie with string (kitchen twine). Roll in flour and sauté in butter until well browned. Add 1 tablespoon flour, broth and catsup, cover pan and cook slowly for 30 minutes.

Remove string before serving.

YIELD: 4 SERVINGS

HOT STRAWBERRY SUNDAE ✤ ✤

By Joe Maciel, Wesport Room manager
Kansas City Union Station

1 pint strawberries, cut in half	no longer need to strain honey)
7 tablespoons rum (Maciel calls for Jamacia Rum)	4 tablespoons lemon juice
¾ cup strained honey (cooks	Rind of 1 orange, cut in strips

Marinate strawberries in rum for 1 hour. Bring honey, lemon juice and orange peel to a boil. Remove orange rind and combine flavored honey with strawberries. Serve immediately over ice cream.

YIELD: 2¼ CUPS

·7·
The World
—— *on* ——
Our Plate

Recipes

150 Years of International Flavors

K-State's homeland, a destination for European and African settlers since before Kansas became a state, is a crazy quilt of cultures. Mexican cowboys, former slaves and German immigrants brought tastes of Spain, Africa, pre-colonial Mexico and Europe with them as they traveled to or through Kansas. Riley County was a gallimaufry of nationalities; in 1890, 1 out of every 10 folks was foreign born.

Like the rest of the country, Kansas food was rooted in the Anglo-Saxon traditions of meat, starch and dessert. Like the rest of the country, pockets of specialized food reflected ethnic differences. But internationalism at K-State goes beyond people trying to recreate the foods from home when they settled Kansas. The influence of worldly cuisines on the college table was marked and early.

Four movements added more pieces to this diverse culinary diorama: the expansion of faculty teaching and research activities, the use of faculty as consultants to overseas institutions, the growth of the international student body and the increase in the number of students traveling to other nations. Each culture, each journey, impacted the K-State table as students and faculty brought to campus their family foodways as well as exotic tastes from faraway places.

Margaret Justin, dean of the College of Home Economics from 1923 to 1954, ca. 1935.
Courtesy of Morse Department of Special Collections, Kansas State University Libraries

Those travels plus the rapidly expanding role of K-State's depth in food production and consumption—growing it and teaching people to use it—cemented the university's foundation in the global community.

As early as 1927 Leo E. Melchers took a leave of absence from his post as head of botany and plant pathology to study problems of plant diseases in Egypt for its government. In the College of Human Ecology, Margaret M. Justin, dean from 1923 to 1954, urged her faculty to work internationally long before it was common. She herself studied at The Hague in the Netherlands on a Fulbright. Martha Kramer chaired home economics in Yenching University, China, for a year; Lucile Rust taught in New Zealand in

1952; Eva McMillan was in Canada, India and Brazil in the 1920s; Abby Marlatt and Vivian Griggs worked in Lebanon. Bessie West set up a department of institutional management at the University of Hawaii in 1938–39 (pre-statehood).

Others became involved in 1954 when the government asked Kansas State, and other land-grant colleges, to help India increase food production. The arrangement continued for 16 years and included faculty members.

James A. McCain, president from 1950 to 1975, called internationalism the university's fourth dimension. He added to resident instruction, research and extension.

Kansas became a forceful player in the global economy as organizations marketed the state's agricultural products. K-State faculty and staff were involved in both marketing and proliferation of products. Interest in all-things international soared.

- In 1920, 20 students from 10 countries were enrolled in KSAC. Thirteen were agriculture majors. International student enrollment climbed to more than 1,850 from 100 plus countries in fall 2011.

- The Cosmopolitan Club, started in 1922, demonstrated an interest on campus in international matters. Playing host to international dinners was one of its activities.

- Between 1965 and 1975, K-State grain and milling scientists developed ties to emerging countries trying to feed their populations.

- By 2010 student study abroad was encouraged for all students and was mandatory for some.

- Faculty on Fulbrights, on sabbaticals and on business, sampled food on six continents.

- Dining services, in efforts to enlighten as well as feed hungry students, sponsored international dinners. Beginning in 1937, *Food for Fifty* carried instructions for preparing "foreign buffets." "American taste is becoming cosmopolitan," wrote authors Sina Faye Fowler and Bessie Brooks West. They offered details on planning and preparing Chinese, Hungarian, Swedish, German and Italian buffet suppers.

- Organizations embraced internationalism with events such as a sorority's Japanese dance featuring a five-course dinner and a four-piece orchestra and the Restaurant Management Club's international dinners in Hoffman Lounge.

The K-State table felt the impact of each step.

A Taste of Argentina

Chef Taji Marie demonstrated this Argentina-inspired dish at the Flavors of Latin America culinary enhancement workshop on campus in 2008. We are including it as a salute to both the international spirit of the annual workshop and the extensive consumer work with beef flavor done by the K-State Sensory Analysis Center. This steak looks beautiful and tastes even better.

GRILLED STEAK WITH CHIMICHURRI ❖❖

From Taji Marie

3–4 pounds flank or rib eye
    steak, room temperature
½ cup parsley
1 cup finely diced white onion
2 cloves garlic, minced
½ cup finely diced red bell
    pepper
¼ cup grated carrots

1 tablespoon dried oregano
1 tablespoon smoked paprika
1 tablespoon salt
1 teaspoon black pepper
½ teaspoon red chili flakes
¼ cup red wine vinegar
¼ cup water
½ cup olive oil

Heat grill to hot.

For the sauce, combine parsley, onion, garlic, bell pepper, carrots, oregano, paprika, salt, pepper, chili flakes, vinegar and water. Stir to combine and set aside at room temperature for 20 to 30 minutes. Add olive oil and taste. Add more salt and pepper as needed.

Grill steaks on both sides to desired temperature. Let rest for 15 minutes before slicing. Serve sauce with sliced meat.

YIELD: 8 SERVINGS

Singapore Curry—The Era that Never Ends

Grace Shugart called it "the Singapore Curry era." For many years, Singapore Curry was featured at the institutional management senior dinner. Bessie Brooks West, the department chair, showed students how to arrange the food on their plates. Merna Zeigler developed the recipe, which Mrs. Shugart adapted to serve at home and added the curried shrimp.

The recipe has been mentioned in every edition of *Food for Fifty*. "It went out of date," said current author Mary Molt, "but Grace Shugart had Singapore Curry parties so it's a nostalgic recipe." Mrs. Shugart served tea and a light dessert, such as sherbet or fruit, with the curry.

Nora Owen Johnson remembers Singapore Curry at her senior dinner in 1954. "It was the first time I ever ate a dish with curry in it. I loved it and still use the recipe," she wrote.

✤✤ SINGAPORE CURRY

From Merna Zeigler and Grace Shugart

CURRIED CHICKEN:

2 (2½ to 3-pound) fryers or chicken pieces (or 1 fryer and 1 pound cubed fresh pork)

¼ cup butter
½ cup flour
4 cups chicken broth
Salt to taste
½ teaspoon curry powder

Cover chicken with salted and seasoned water and cook until tender. Remove from water and cool. Remove meat from bones and cut into bite-sized pieces. Heat butter in medium-sized sauce pan. Add flour and cook, stirring until mixture is bubbly. Add broth and continue stirring until mixture resembles a cream sauce. Salt to taste and season with curry powder. The amount of curry may need to be adjusted. The sauce should have a distinctive yellow color. Carefully stir in chicken.

CURRIED SHRIMP:

6 tablespoons butter or margarine

6 tablespoons flour

1 teaspoon salt

3 cups milk

½ teaspoon curry powder

2 pounds shrimp, cleaned and cooked

1 pound fresh mushrooms, sliced and sautéed

Heat butter in medium-sized sauce pan. Add flour and cook, stirring until mixture is bubbly. Add salt and milk. Continue stirring until mixture resembles a cream sauce. Add curry powder and adjust seasonings, if needed. Add shrimp and mushrooms. Heat thoroughly.

ACCOMPANIMENTS:

12 servings French fried onion rings

4 to 5 tomatoes, sliced

4 to 5 bananas, cut into chunks

2 (20-ounce) cans pineapple chunks

1 cup coconut

1 cup salted or dry roasted peanuts

1 (10 to 12-ounce) jar chutney (such as Major Grey's)

8 cups cooked rice

To serve, arrange foods on a buffet table in the following order: rice, curried chicken, curried shrimp, onion rings, tomatoes, bananas, pineapple, coconut, peanuts and chutney.

Each guest takes a serving of rice and then pours the curried meat of his choice over the rice and tops with accompaniments as desired.

YIELD: 10 to 12 GENEROUS SERVINGS

Smokey Flavors with Marmalade from Spain

Missy Schrader, a dietitian with Kansas State Housing and Dining Services and instructor in hospitality management and dietetics, created the Culinary Enhancement Workshop series in 2005. For that she received national honors from the American Dietetic Association Foundation for innovative food and culinary effort. The workshops, now in their 9th year, bring in a nationally recognized chef for a daylong event for food service professionals, alumni, community members and students.

This is one of the recipes Schrader prepares most often from all those distributed to participants at the annual workshops. It came from Taji Marie, a California chef featured at Flavors of the Mediterranean, the 2007 workshop in Derby Dining Center. Schrader serves it with apricot and almond couscous.

✣✣ GRILLED SMOKEY PORK SKEWERS WITH GARLIC-ONION MARMALADE
From Taji Marie

---

1 tablespoon smoked paprika (mild pimenton)	½ teaspoon ground pepper
1 teaspoon ground cumin	Olive oil
¼ teaspoon red chili flakes	1 pound pork tenderloin, cut into 1-inch cubes
2 cloves garlic, minced	Bamboo skewers, soaked in water for 30 minutes
¾ teaspoon salt	

Heat grill to hot.

In a medium bowl, combine the paprika, cumin, chili flakes, garlic, salt and pepper. Add enough olive oil to create a paste. Add the cubed pork and toss to coat well. Thread pork onto bamboo skewers.

Place the skewers on a hot grill and cook on all sides until well marked and just cooked through. Serve warm with Garlic-Onion Marmalade.

GARLIC-ONION MARMALADE

2 tablespoons olive oil	¼ teaspoon allspice
5 garlic cloves, thinly sliced	¼ cup golden raisins
1 red onion, sliced into thin half circles	¼ cup water
	Sherry vinegar
Juice and zest of 2 oranges	Salt
1 tablespoon sugar	

In a medium saucepan, combine the olive oil, garlic and onions. Heat over medium-high heat. Cook until onions are soft. Add the orange zest and juice, sugar, allspice, raisins and water. Simmer for about 15 minutes or until onions are very soft and liquid is thickened. Remove from heat. Add a splash of sherry vinegar and taste. Adjust seasoning with salt and more vinegar, if needed. Serve at room temperature.

YIELD: 6 SERVINGS

ELIZABETH EDWARDS

Seventeen-year-old Elizabeth Edwards (Harley) came to K-State in 1886 from Wales. She was the first woman international student to attend KSAC. It is believed that she churned the first butter ever made on campus in a dairying course. She graduated in 1892.

Sensory Experiences from Thailand and India

Edgar and Delores Chambers travel the world in their roles as leaders of K-State's Sensory Analysis Center, which has satellites at K-State Olathe and in Thailand. He is a university distinguished professor in human nutrition; she is professor in the same department in human ecology.

These are two of her favorite international recipes. The popular Palak Paneer, a delicacy from northern India, was given to her by Uma Chitra, a Fulbright Scholar in 2009–2010 at Kansas State who is head of nutrition and dietetics at Kasturba Gandhi Degree and PG College in Secunderabad, India.

✤✤ PALAK PANEER

From Uma Chitra

10 ounces baby spinach leaves	1 teaspoon minced garlic
¼ cup vegetable oil	1–2 teaspoons ginger paste
8 ounces paneer cheese, cubed	1 teaspoon coriander powder
½ teaspoon cumin seeds	Chili powder to taste
1 red onion, peeled and minced in a food processor	Paprika to taste
	Salt to taste

Blanch spinach and drain. When cool, puree in food processor.

Heat oil in a non-stick pan. Lightly fry the paneer cubes to a golden brown color. Drain on absorbent paper.

In the same pan, heat oil and add cumin seeds, onion, and garlic. Sauté until brown. Add ginger paste, coriander, chili powder and paprika. Add spinach and season to taste with salt. Adjust seasonings.

Toss in the fried paneer cubes. Serve hot with fried rice or Naan bread.

YIELD: 4 SERVINGS

GREEN PAPAYA SALAD ✤ ✤

From Delores Chambers

1 cup green papaya, peeled
and shredded

3 cloves garlic, peeled and
minced

5 fresh green beans, cut into
1 inch pieces

2 tomatoes, diced

2 tablespoons dried shrimp

2 tablespoons Tai fish sauce

2 tablespoons freshly squeezed
lime juice

1 tablespoon granulated sugar

1 tablespoon roasted peanuts,
coarsely chopped

Combine papaya, garlic, green beans, tomatoes and dried shrimp.

Mix the fish sauce, lime juice and sugar until the sugar has dissolved. Pour over the papaya mixture.

Sprinkle with nuts.

YIELD: 2 SERVINGS

Student Contributes Taste of Japan

This recipe from student Emiko Taki was published in the delightful "Food for Five" booklet, a 1984 project of students, faculty, alumni and friends of the Department of Dietetics, Restaurant and Institutional Management (now Hospitality Management and Dietetics).

Playing off the title *Food for Fifty*, the group dedicated their collection of "tried and true" recipes to Grace Shugart who was author for many years of *Food for Fifty*. There were 78 contributors and several of their recipes, including these two Asian classics, are used in this book.

❖❖ PORK SATAY

From Emiko Taki, Student Dietetic Association

---

2 cloves garlic	½ cup soy sauce
½ cup chopped green onions	2 teaspoons coriander powder
1 tablespoon chopped fresh ginger root	1 teaspoon red pepper flakes
1 cup roasted peanuts	½ cup chicken broth
2 tablespoons lemon juice	½ cup melted butter
2 tablespoons honey	1½ pounds pork tenderloin, cut into 1-inch cubes

---

In a food processor, puree garlic, green onions, ginger, peanuts, lemon juice, honey, soy sauce, coriander and red pepper flakes until almost smooth. Pour in broth and butter. Pulse a few times until well mixed.

Place pork cubes in a large resealable plastic bag and pour mixture over meat. Marinate in the refrigerator for 6 hours or overnight.

Drain meat and set aside, reserving marinade. Pour marinade into a small saucepan; boil for 5 minutes. Reserve a small amount of the marinade for basting, and set the remainder aside to serve as a dipping sauce.

Preheat grill for medium heat. Thread pork cubes onto bamboo skewers that have been soaked in water for 30 minutes.

Lightly oil preheated grill. Grill meat for 10 to 15 minutes or until well browned, turning and brushing frequently with cooked marinade. Serve with dipping sauce.

YIELD: 4 SERVINGS

Winning Mexican Soup Recipe from Dining Services

Fern Mayfield, recipe development coordinator for dining services, created this Mexican-inspired soup. The recipe won first place in a national competition sponsored by the Campbell Soup Company in 1995.

CHICKEN ENCHILADA SOPA ✧ ✧

From Fern Mayfield, K-State Dining Services

2 tablespoons butter or margarine

1 medium onion, chopped

2 cloves garlic, minced

3 (14.5-ounce) cans chicken broth

3 cups crushed tortilla chips

3 cups cooked, diced chicken

2 (4-ounce) cans diced green chilies

1 (10-ounce) can diced tomatoes and green chilies or 1¼ cups salsa

1 cup sour cream

¼ cup fresh minced cilantro

Mozzarella cheese, shredded

Cheddar cheese, shredded

Melt butter in a Dutch oven over medium heat. Add onions and garlic, stirring until fragrant. Add broth and bring to a boil. Add crushed chips. Remove from heat, cover and let stand for 10 minutes to dissolve chips. Stir as needed.

Add chicken, chilies and tomatoes (or salsa) to broth/tortilla chip mixture. Cook over medium heat until thoroughly heated, but do not allow to boil. Remove from heat. Stir in sour cream and cilantro.

Serve immediately. Sprinkle each serving with mozzarella and cheddar cheeses.

YIELD: 8 (1-CUP) SERVINGS

Students from Ecuador showcased their country's cuisine at a 2013 coffee hour sponsored by International Student and Scholar Services. COURTESY OF DAVID MAYES, KANSAS STATE UNIVERSITY DIVISION OF COMMUNICATIONS AND MARKETING

Feasts and Festivals

Students representing more than 100 countries make up the International Coordinating Council. The council's annual International Week usually has at least one food event. In 1973, the Feast of Nations Committee collected recipes for a booklet and in 1994, the International Week Food Committee compiled one, too.

Although the recipe is titled coconut cake, it tastes like a macaroon cookie casserole. Try serving it with a dab of freshly whipped cream and strawberries.

PASTEL DE COCO ✤ ✤

From Feast of Nations Committee World Cookbook *(1973)*

---

4 eggs

1 can sweetened condensed milk

1½ cups coconut

½ cup raisins

¼ teaspoon baking powder

1 teaspoon vanilla

Preheat oven to 350°F.

Beat eggs. Add milk, coconut, raisins, baking powder and vanilla. Mix well. Pour into 9 x 13-inch pan. Bake for 40 minutes or until knife inserted into center comes out clean.

YIELD: 20 SERVINGS

·8·
Writing
—— *on* ——
the Table

Recipes

"Today I hear much criticism regarding food in the Middle West. The complaints come usually from tourists who pass through at sixty miles an hour eating en route in public places, and seldom at the best. I doubt these scorners have ever sat down as a guest at a family table. True, the food of the plains country is forthright...but for the most part it is wholesome and well cooked... It is food to be eaten with real enjoyment."

Clementine Paddleford
April 20, 1952 issue of *This Week* magazine
(Box 73 in the Paddleford Collection at Kansas State University)

Who Wrote That Recipe?

Standing between the farmer and the cook, more times than not, is a person with a reporter's notebook. These food writers and journalists advise, guide, inform and entertain those of us who put soupspoon to mouth and those of us who put soup on the table.

A handful of these food missionaries have K-State roots. Most famous, and probably most prominent of the bunch, is Clementine Paddleford, a 1921 industrial journalism graduate. During her career she was called the world's most influential food writer.

Nell Nichols edited more than a dozen *Farm Journal* cookbooks. Jane Butel introduced Southwestern cuisine into the national landscape where it took root and thrived. Michael Bauer influences food journalism throughout the country. Janet Helm advocates for dietitians and for healthy eating.

There were Kathleen Kelly, an "icon in Kansas journalism" who wrote about food for the *Wichita Eagle-Beacon* for 40 years; Betty Lou Denton, former home editor of *Kansas Farmer Magazine* and food editor of the *Topeka Capital-Journal* (1958–64) in Topeka and former president of the American Agricultural Editors Association; and Sue Morgan Dawson who retired as food editor of the *Columbus (Ohio) Dispatch*.

These journalists didn't just kiss the cook. With their words, they embraced, appreciated and led the cook on adventures.

Clementine Paddleford, the Most Influential Food Writer of her Time

The hometown of Clementine Paddleford, whose food-writing career ran from 1936 to 1967, drowned under the waters of Tuttle Creek Reservoir. Like the little town of Stockdale, Paddleford had nearly disappeared from the American mind until the K-State library revived interest in her. At one time she had an estimated 12 million readers.

A symposium in 2005, on the anniversary of her birthday, celebrated Paddleford and the collection she bequeathed to Hale Library's Morse Department of Special Collections. The event spawned a story in the *New York Times* by A. J. Apple, a seasoned political and international journalist turned food writer. His story, "The Most Famous Food Writer You Never Heard Of," kindled a spark that became a fire.

In *Saveur* magazine Kelly Alexander wrote, "Paddleford was arguably the first journalist to call attention to the fact that there is a rich tradition of good eating on these [American] shores – a tradition worth preserving and building on. And it all started in Kansas."

Alexander and Cynthia Harris collaborated on *Hometown Appetites*, a biography of the food journalist published by Gotham in 2008. Ms. Harris curated the entire Paddleford collection—all 363 plus boxes of it, a job that took 3½ years. She is arguably the world's expert on the K-State graduate.

Clem's scrapbook from her days in Wildcat country, nestled in Paddleford Box 316, is filled with clever notes from friends, party invitations, photographs and menus. They offer a peek at the indomitable spirit who was to become became such a force in the food world.

Clementine Paddleford, ca. 1921.
COURTESY OF MORSE DEPARTMENT OF SPECIAL COLLECTIONS, KANSAS STATE UNIVERSITY LIBRARIES

In 1924 she was women's editor of *Farm and Fireside* in New York. Before her death in 1967 she wrote for the *New York Herald Tribune*, the *World Journal Tribune*, *This Week* magazine and *Gourmet* magazine. She wrote several cookbooks and a small stirring tribute to her mother called *A Flower for My Mother*. *How America Eats* was published in 1960 by Charles Scribner's Sons and included material from Paddleford's work for *This Week* and the *Herald Tribune*.

Her columns exemplified Paddleford's passion for food and for adventure. She loved to travel and often flew a Piper Cub to relax from her hectic work pace. She was powerfully curious, ferreting out stories aboard submarines, at Spanish olive harvests, during Queen Elizabeth II's coronation celebrations in 1953, and in Kansas farmhouses.

Her distinctive writing style—sentences were often just phrases—and her appetite for chronicling real people's tables were trademarks that set her apart. That curiosity and fearless grit surely came from her grandfather, Stephen Decatur Paddleford, who moved his wife and three children to a Kansas homestead. Her parents farmed south of Stockdale and Paddleford grew up amid farmwomen feeding their families at the whim of nature. Her mother Jennie had taken some of the earliest domestic sciences K-State offered in 1883, but she left after two years to teach school.

Jennie Romick Paddleford taught her daughter many lessons, including the joy of feeding the family and eating together. But the most impressionable one was "Never grow a wishbone where your backbone ought to be." Although she lived in New York City and traveled the world, Clementine Paddleford never forgot that backbone and she never forgot her Kansas roots. "There is no perfume in the world like the springtime smell of prairie air," she wrote.

In *A Flower for My Mother*, she wrote, "It was in a yellow limestone church at Stockdale, Kansas, a crossroads town, that I sat dreaming during summer Sunday sermons, not of heaven or hell, but of the good dinner to come." To her, Sunday dinner symbolized good food that was home grown, home cooked and seasonal.

She also wrote about a Kansas strawberry social, her family cranking the ice cream freezer to make strawberry ice cream. The freezer was then carried to the cellar to let the ice cream ripen, then hauled to the June festival to sell for 10 cents a dish. Proceeds went to pay the preacher.

"Tongues grew warm with the friction of friendly chatter," she wrote in the column about strawberry shortcake that tasted "of sugar and sun."

Clementine Paddleford helped a nations document and appreciate its culinary heritage, 1961. COURTESY OF MORSE DEPARTMENT OF SPECIAL COLLECTIONS, KANSAS STATE UNIVERSITY LIBRARIES

❖❖ OLD-FASHIONED STRAWBERRY SHORTCAKE

From Clementine Paddleford

3 cups all-purpose flour
5 teaspoons baking powder
⅛ teaspoon grated nutmeg
1 teaspoon salt
1 cup sugar, divided, plus
    more to taste

½ cup (1 stick) plus 2
    tablespoons unsalted
    butter, chilled and cut
    into small pieces
1 large egg, beaten
½ cup milk
3 quarts ripe fresh strawberries
Whipped cream, optional

Preheat the oven to 400°F.

Sift the flour, baking powder, nutmeg, salt and ½ cup of the sugar into a large bowel. Transfer to a food processor, add ½ cup of the butter and pulse until the mixture resembles coarse meal. Transfer the dough back to the bowl. Add egg and milk. Knead the dough very gently with your fingertips or spatula until it holds together, about 10 seconds. Dots of butter should be visible. Generously flour work surface and roll the dough out on it to form 2 circles that are ½ inch thick and 8 to 10 inches in diameter. Wrap the disks tightly in plastic and refrigerate.

Set aside 16 of the best-looking strawberries. Hull and halve the rest, and place in a bowl with the remaining ½ cup sugar or more, depending on the ripeness of the fruit. Let the strawberries macerate for 15 to 45 minutes.

Remove the dough disks from the refrigerator. Place the dough disks on 2 ungreased sheet pans and bake for 12 to 15 minutes, until golden on the outside and just cooked through in the center. Remove from the oven and cool for 10 to 15 minutes.

Slather the remaining 2 tablespoons butter evenly over the disks. Transfer 1 disk to a plate that will accommodate it and the juicy berries running off it. Pile the macerated berries on top and then cover with the other biscuit. Garnish with the reserved whole berries and serve with whipped cream, if you like.

Yield: 8 servings

On September 21, 1952, in *This Week*, Paddleford wrote (Box 74, Folder 20) about memories of box socials, Sunday night suppers and walnut cake. Black walnuts were Kansas. Still are. Kansas is the nation's top producer. They were so plentiful some cooks even canned them!

Ashley Miller, who got her master's degree in sensory analysis at K-State in 2012, tested cultivars of black walnuts to help growers understand consumer preferences and to set a standard for food manufacturers who use black walnuts in their products.

BLACK WALNUT CAKE ✤✤

From Clementine Paddleford

½ cup unsalted butter, softened
1½ cups sugar
2 cups all-purpose flour
4 teaspoons baking powder
½ teaspoon salt

1 cup milk
1 cup finely ground black walnuts
1 teaspoon vanilla
4 egg whites
¼ teaspoon cream of tartar

Preheat the oven to 325°F. Grease and flour a 9-inch tube pan.

In a large bowl using an electric mixer, cream the butter and sugar well. Sift the flour, baking powder and salt into a medium bowl. Add the flour mixture to the creamed mixture alternately with the milk, mixing well after each addition. Stir in the walnuts and vanilla.

In a medium bowl, beat the egg whites until foamy. Add the cream of tartar and continue beating until stiff peaks form. Fold the egg whites into the butternut mixture.

Pour the batter into the prepared pan and bake for 15 minutes or until the cake begins to rise. Increase the oven temperature to 350°F and bake for 30 to 40 minutes longer, until a wooden skewer inserted into the center comes out clean.

Cool the cake in the pan on a wire rack for 30 minutes, then invert the cake onto the rack, remove the pan and cool completely. Serve the cake at room temperature with whipped cream or ice cream, if you like.

YIELD: 12 TO 14 SERVINGS

Nell Nichols Gathered Farm Recipes from Sea to Shining Sea

As editor at the *Farm Journal*, headquartered in Philadelphia, Nell Nichols had her hands on more than a dozen cookbooks. Like Paddleford, whom she knew, Nichols collected, listed, and published recipes from many sources. Hers were mostly from *Farm Journal* readers.

Nell Beaunbien Nichols grew up on a ranch near Dodge City. Her high school class had 12 students; she studied Latin and German. She graduated from K-State in 1916 with a degree in home economics. She wanted to combine nutrition and journalism so headed to the University of Wisconsin, Madison.

One of her professors was Abby Lillian Marlatt who earned degrees at K-State in 1888 and 1890; the professor's father was Washington Marlatt, early Manhattan settler and a founder of Bluemont Central College, the forerunner of K-State. In an oral history in the UW archives, Nichols calls Marlett one of her most interesting professors.

Nichols returned to Kansas to marry in 1917 and, when her husband went to war, she was offered a job in journalism at UW for $100 a month. She supplemented her income by selling food stories to magazines.

She returned to Topeka and continued to freelance. *Farm and Fireside* magazine hired her as field editor in 1920. In 1923 she published *The Farm Cook and Rule Book* which included recipes, nutritional information, a special section on cooking for the sick and a beauty secrets section, revealing information she learned from interviewing older farmwomen. She joined the staff of *Women's Home Companion* in 1929.

Then she joined *Farm Journal* where she was food editor for four years. She became the cookbook editor, developing recipes from reader contributions and her own experiences eating in homes and restaurants. Her books reveal the history of the rural kitchen, from equipment to tastes, from availability of food to cultural changes. These are only two of the thousands of recipes she put before the American cook. Another recipe from Nichols is Roasted Raccoon, page 17.

About the apple butter she wrote: "Grandmother made apple butter for two important reasons that are just as valid today: it tastes exceptionally good and it makes use of the sound parts of culls or windfalls. Once apple butter cooked for long hours in big black kettles over fires built in the yard. Someone had to stir it constantly so neighbors came over to take their turns at the stirring and to visit."

The *Farm Journal* version needs to be stirred only once every half hour. Although any apples can be transformed into apple butter, many recommend Granny Smith. The lemon cookie recipe was one of the *Farm Journal*'s most requested recipes.

OVEN APPLE BUTTER ❖ ❖

From Farm Journal's Country Cookbook *(1959)*

2 quarts water	3½–4 cups sugar
2 tablespoons salt	1 teaspoon ground cinnamon
6 pounds apples, cored, peeled, and sliced	½ teaspoon ground cloves
	½ teaspoon ground allspice
2 quarts sweet cider	

Combine water and salt. Add apples. Drain well but do not rinse slices.
Put through food chopper, using finest blade. Measure pulp and juice.
There should be 2 quarts.

Combine with cider. Place in large oven (350°F). Let mixture simmer
about 3 to 3½ hours until cooked down about half and is thick and mushy.
Stir thoroughly every half hour.

Put mixture through sieve or food mill; it should yield 2¼ to 2½ quarts.

Combine sugar and spices; add to sauce and return to oven. Continue
simmering about 1½ hours or until thick, stirring every half hour. To test, pour
small amount onto cold plate. If no liquid oozes around edge, apple butter is cooked.

Pour into hot jars; adjust lids and process in boiling water bath (212°F) for 10
minutes. Remove jars and complete seals unless closures are self-sealing kind or
keep in refrigerator.

YIELD: 2 QUARTS

❖❖ LEMON COCONUT SQUARES

From Farm Journal's Country Cookbook *(1959)*

COOKIE DOUGH:

1½ cups sifted flour

½ cup brown sugar, firmly packed

½ cup butter or margarine

1 cup chopped nuts

2 tablespoons flour

½ teaspoon baking powder

¼ teaspoon salt

½ teaspoon vanilla

FILLING:

2 eggs, beaten

1 cup brown sugar, firmly packed

1½ cups flaked or shredded coconut

FROSTING:

1 cup confectioners' sugar

1 tablespoon melted butter or margarine

Juice of 1 lemon (4 tablespoons)

Preheat oven to 275°F. Butter 13 x 9 x 2-inch pan.

Mix together flour, brown sugar, and butter for cookie dough; pat down well in prepared pan. Bake for 10 minutes or until dough sets.

Turn oven to 350°F.

To make filling, combine eggs, sugar, coconut, nuts, flour, baking powder, salt and vanilla. Spread on top of baked mixture. Bake at 350°F for 20 minutes.

As cookies bake, combine confectioners' sugar, melted butter and lemon juice. Remove cookies from oven and spread frosting over warm cookies. Cool slightly and cut in 2-inch squares. Remove from pan and continue to cool on baking racks.

YIELD: 24 COOKIES

Kathleen Kelly—Expanding the World of Food in Kansas

A fresh K-State degree in home economics and journalism in hand, Kathleen Kelly went to work for the *Wichita Eagle-Beacon* in 1955. She called herself the *Eagle*'s home economist and stayed there for 40 years, reporting on cooks, ingredients, culinary techniques and the cuisine of Kansas.

She was called "an exuberant spirit" and an "icon in Kansas journalism."

She retired from journalism in 1995, telling her *Wichita Eagle* readers: "We've broken bread, harvested persimmons, licked bowls, stuffed sausage, tied comforters. …We've explored whipped cream and chocolate, organ meats and oat bran, with equal abandon. …We've traveled the world and, best of all, we've gotten into the nooks and crannies of Kansas." She died in 2012 at age 76.

"She brought a lot of culture to the Plains," wrote coworker Fran Kentling. Kelly traveled to cooking schools in Paris

Kathleen Kelly, center, works with classmates on a course called Home Page. It was taught by Helen Hostetter who was the first woman to be named full professor of journalism in the U.S. She retired in 1964 after 30 years at K-State. COURTESY OF KELLY HUMPHRIES

and Hong Kong, learned about Thai cooking in Bangkok and spent days with Simone Beck in France. From each journey she brought back recipes to her Kansas readers.

Near the end of her career Kelly became enamored with cattle drive cooking, according to her son Kelly Humphries who works at the Johnson Space Center in Houston and tells wonderful tales about growing up with a food editor mom.

Kelly wrote, in *Favorite Recipes, 35 Years of Kansas Prizewinners from the Wichita Eagle*, that this pickle recipe from a 1989 Sunday Fare column was one of the paper's most requested.

✤✤ EXCELLENT MICROWAVE PICKLES

From Kathleen Kelly

½ teaspoon salt	1 cup sugar
¼ teaspoon turmeric	2 cucumbers, unpeeled,
¼ teaspoon mustard seed	thinly sliced
¼ teaspoon celery seed	1 or 2 onions, thinly sliced
½ cup vinegar	

In small bowl combine salt, turmeric, mustard seed, celery seed, vinegar and sugar. Mix cucumbers and onions in large microwave-safe bowl. Pour vinegar mixture over cucumbers and onions. Microwave, uncovered, on high for 5 minutes. Stir well; return to microwave for 5 more minutes. Cool. Pour in quart jar and refrigerate. Pickles are ready to eat when thoroughly chilled. Store in refrigerator.

YIELD: 1 QUART

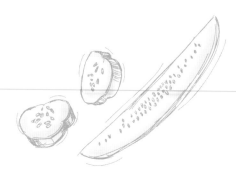

Pioneers called rhubarb "pie plant." A common ingredient in many Kansas gardens, it is most often made into cobblers, crisps and pie.

SWEET AND SOUR RHUBARB BREAD ✥ ✥

From Kathleen Kelly

2¾ cups flour	1 teaspoon vanilla
1½ cups packed brown sugar	1 cup finely chopped rhubarb
1 teaspoon baking soda	(if frozen, thaw and drain)
1 teaspoon salt	2 tablespoons flour, additional
1 egg	2 tablespoons butter
1 cup buttermilk	2 tablespoons sugar
½ cup vegetable oil	¼ cup chopped nuts

Preheat oven to 350°F. Grease two 8 x 4 x 2-inch loaf pans.

In large mixing bowl stir together 2¾ cups flour, brown sugar, baking soda and salt. In another bowl combine egg, buttermilk, oil and vanilla. Stir into dry ingredients, mixing well.

Toss rhubarb with 2 tablespoons flour and fold into batter. Pour into prepared pans. Dot each loaf with butter and sprinkle with sugar and nuts.

Bake for about 50 minutes or until wooden toothpick inserted in the center comes out clean. Cool in pans for 10 minutes then remove and cool on wire rack. Serve warm with cream cheese.

Yield: 2 loaves

Michael Bauer—Trend Spotter, Restaurant Critic, Leader in Modern Food Journalism

Michael Bauer, who earned a master's degree from the journalism department in 1975, is executive food and wine editor and restaurant critic at the *San Francisco Chronicle* where he is responsible for the largest food and wine staff of any newspaper in the United States. During his career he and his words and recipes have influenced millions of readers and his blog, which he started in 1996—"musings on food & wine"—added to his readership.

His most enduring legacy, besides making every other American food editor green with envy, is his impact on food journalism. He is a founder and past president of the Association of Food Journalists and has helped reporters and food experts polish their writing and reporting skills.

One of those is Kim Severson who became the dining writer at the *New York Times*. "Those of us who went through the House of Bauer learned many things," she said. "For one, the importance of journalistic integrity when writing about food. Michael was instrumental in designing the ethical guidelines for food critics that were adopted by the Association of Food Journalists and are widely considered the standard in the industry. He also insisted recipes needed to be as thoroughly reported and tested as a news story."

She added: "All in all, Michael is a visionary when it comes to food journalism, and he has a palate that won't quit. He can spot a trend before it breaks, and has the creativity and determination to turn his hunch about a coming trend into a great newspaper package. He was one of the most influential food writers and editors through the 1990s and into the 2000s."

Bauer came from a food background—he worked at his father's meat market in Chanute—but he never thought food would be his life. "As a starving student working on a graduate degree in a short-lived program called Mental Health Mass Communications, food wasn't the center of my universe."

At the *Kansas City Star*, he wrote about behavioral sciences before switching to food. "I fell in love with the topic," he said. He went to the *Dallas Times Herald* then to San Francisco in 1996. In 2004 he was inducted into the James Beard Foundation's Who's Who of Food and Beverage in America. "It's strange how things catch up with you. You feel as if you grow and change, but I learned that what I learned in Kansas still informs what I do in San Francisco," he wrote.

Bauer's surprising recipe pick for this book deserves an explanation. "Of course anyone who grew up in the Midwest knows about the Chex Party Mix, but living in one of the food capitals of the United States I figured I'd moved far beyond this homey treat," he wrote. "About 15 years ago I found my mother's original recipe, adapted it a bit, and made up a batch for a story we were doing at *The Chronicle* on retro food. It was designed to be a joke. My colleagues laughed, and then they ate. And ate. And ate. My Chex Mix recipe has now become a tradition at our annual Christmas party we throw for about 100 friends and colleagues. Sophisticated? Maybe not, but good always wins out."

MICHAEL BAUER'S CHEX PARTY MIX ✤✤

7 cups Rice Chex (7 ounces)

7 cups Wheat Chex
(11 ounces)

7 cups Corn Chex (7 ounces)

1 (15-ounce) box Cheerios

1 (9-ounce) package thin
pretzels

1 (12½-ounce) can Spanish
peanuts

⅓ cup bacon grease

½ cup margarine or butter

2 tablespoons Tabasco

1 heaping teaspoon chili
powder (with salt)

Preheat oven to 200°F. Mix the cereals, pretzels and peanuts together in a large roasting pan and set aside. Melt together the bacon grease, margarine and Tabasco and stir into the dry ingredients. Sprinkle on the chili powder and stir again.

Bake for 2 hours, stirring every 20 minutes.

Yield: 50 cups

Jane Butel, The Chile Queen

After graduating with a degree in home economics and journalism in 1959 and holding hefty positions such as vice president for American Express in New York, Jane Butel became a devotee of the chile and its accompanying cuisines.

Jane Butel has written more than 20 cookbooks on Southwestern and Mexican regional cuisine.
COURTESY OF JANE BUTEL

Often credited with nationalizing the Southwestern cooking craze, she has written 20 cookbooks such as *Real Women Eat Chiles* and *Chili Madness: A Passionate Cookbook*. She started Pecos Valley Spice Company in 1978 and operates a cooking school in Corrales, New Mexico.

Another Butel specialty—and cookbook topic—is cuisine from regional Mexico. She has also written extensively on Tex-Mex, one of the few cuisines originating in the United States.

Jane Butel says this recipe has won chili cook-offs and was inspired by her maternal grandfather who learned to make chili from trail cooks. It is one of her trademark recipes. She taught it at the Department of Hospitality Management and Dietetics' annual culinary workshop in 2010. She has donated her professional papers to Richard L. D. and Marjorie J. Morse Department of Special Collections at Hale Library.

PECOS RIVER BOWL O'RED ✤✤

By Jane Butel

2 tablespoons lard, butter, bacon
   drippings or rendered beef fat
1 large onion, coarsely chopped
3 pounds lean beef, cut into
   ½-inch cubes
3 medium-size garlic cloves,
   finely chopped

¼ cup ground hot chile or to taste
¼ cup ground mild chile
1 tablespoon ground cumin
About 3 cups water
1½ teaspoons salt or to taste

Heat lard in a large heavy pot over medium heat. Add onion and cook until softened. Remove from heat.

Add meat, garlic, ground chiles and cumin to pot. Break up any lumps. Stir in the water and salt. Return to heat. Bring to a boil, then reduce heat and simmer, uncovered, 2½ to 3 hours, stirring occasionally, until the meat is very tender and the flavors are well blended. Add more water if necessary. Taste and adjust seasonings.

YIELD: 6 SERVINGS

Shirley Sarvis—A Food and Wine Pioneer

Shirley Sarvis, who graduated from K-State in home economics in 1957, was a food writer, cookbook author and an acknowledged pioneer in the art of food and wine pairing. She critically examined why food and wine matched, or didn't. She died in 2013 in San Francisco.

She understood, one writer explained, that wine is not about pretentiousness but that it is "there to help us slow down and get in touch with our souls."

A San Francisco chef said of her talent: "She had a really rare palate—out there in the stratosphere—in terms of her ability to taste."

Ms. Sarvis was born in Norton in 1935. She worked for *Sunset* magazine between 1957 and 1962 and then freelanced for *Travel and Leisure*, *Woman's Day*, *Food and Wine*, *Gourmet* and other magazines. She worked on about a dozen cookbooks over the years. She counted Julia and Paul Child among her friends.

Food and wine paring pioneer Shirley Sarvis at Fournou's Ovens, San Francisco, where she did many wine paring luncheons, ca. 1980. COURTESY OF KRISTINA HALL, SARVIS ESTATE

Sarvis developed both these recipes for Sanford Winery in Lompoc, California. The steak pairs with Pinot Noir, La Rinconada Vineyard, Sanford, 2000. "These herbs echo, remarkably, the aged taste of the fine beef. In dry form, the thyme and sage give a nutty taste that helps to show off the rich Pinot Noir fruit of the wine," she wrote. She suggested serving the steak with "hot cooked tender cannelloni or small white beans or baked potatoes. Season either with additional herb butter if you wish."

She developed the Lime Avocado Salad to pair with Vin Gris Pinot Noir, Sanford, 2001. Both recipes are printed here as she wrote them.

NEW YORK STEAK WITH THYME-SAGE GLOSS ✧ ✧

From Shirley Sarvis

1 tablespoon very soft unsalted
   butter
¼ teaspoon each crumbled dry
   thyme and sage (or minced
   leaves of fresh herbs)
Salt
Freshly ground quality white
   pepper

1 teaspoon fresh lemon juice
½ teaspoon finely chopped parsley
1 very well aged prime New
   York steak about ¾ pound
   and 1¼ inches thick, near
   room temperature
Clarified butter if needed★

Stir together with a fork butter, thyme, sage, a few grains of salt, a grinding
of pepper, lemon juice and parsley. Trim excess fat from meat. Wipe meat dry.
Season well with salt and pepper. Sprinkle bottom of a heavy frying pan with
salt (preferably coarse). Heat over high heat. Add steak. Brown well on one side;
turn and brown on second side, continuing to cook, lowering heat and turning
occasionally until rare, about 4 minutes total. (Add clarified butter to prevent
overbrowning.) Remove from pan. Let stand 2 minutes. Slice thinly across the
grain. Lift to serving plates, adding juices. Spread herb butter over.

YIELD: 2 SERVINGS

★CLARIFIED BUTTER: Heat a quantity of unsalted butter in a small heavy pan
over low heat to slowly melt. Remove from heat, tilt pan, and discard foam on
top. Spoon or pour out the pure golden clarified butter from the milky residue
settled at the bottom of the pan.

❖❖ BRIGHT LIME AVOCADO SALAD

From Shirley Sarvis

Tender frisée separated into
single-stem short leaves
to measure about 1 cup
(loosely pack to measure)
Lime dressing (recipe below)
1 small avocado, peeled and
thinly sliced lengthwise
2 small prime ripe tomatoes,
halved from top to bottom
and thinly sliced crosswise
About 2 tablespoons cilantro
(fresh coriander) leaves
(no stems)

2 tablespoons finely chopped
very fresh natural pecans
Small-lime halves or larger-
lime wedges to garnish

LIME DRESSING:
4 tablespoons olive oil
1½ tablespoons fresh
lime juice
½ teaspoon salt
A grinding of white pepper

Whisk together all ingredients.

Turn frisée with a small amount of dressing and arrange loosely on two large plates. Arrange avocado slices, slightly overlapping, over frisée. Arrange tomato slices similarly. Sprinkle both lightly with salt, and spoon dressing generously over. Sprinkle cilantro leaves over all. Garnish with limes.

YIELD: 2 LUNCHEON SERVINGS

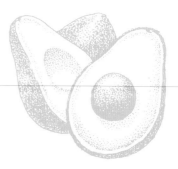

Janet Helm, an Advocate for Dietitians and Healthy Food Choices

Janet Helm combined degrees in journalism and dietetics to create a career as a nutrition communicator. The registered dietitian is chief food and nutrition strategist in North America for Weber Shandwick, a global public relations firm for the of food and beverage industry.

Helm received a bachelor's degree in human ecology and mass communication in 1979 and a master of science in dietetics and institutional management in 1984. "My passion," she says, "is translating nutrition science into intelligible words and healthy food choices."

She wrote *The Food Lover's Healthy Habits Cookbook* and founded the Nutrition Blog Network for dietitians. She blogs at nutritionunplugged.com.

This classic Lebanese dip has become Helm's go-to appetizer at parties. "Even though I like the plain garlic-lemony version best, I'll often experiment by adding different ingredients including canned chipotle in sauce, roasted red peppers, chopped jalapeno, olives, cilantro or pomegranate molasses," she says. "My Lebanese mother-in-law will boil the canned chickpeas first to soften and get rid of the thin skin on the bean (to make for a really creamy hummus), but I will often skip this step."

HUMMUS ✤ ✤

From Janet Helm

4 cloves garlic, peeled halved
2 (16-ounce) cans of chickpeas, drained and rinsed
⅔ cup tahini, well stirred
Juice of 2 lemons
1 teaspoon salt
¼ cup olive oil
water (as needed)
Optional garnish: whole chickpeas, toasted pine nuts, chopped parsley, paprika, cumin or sumac

Combine garlic, chickpeas, tahini, lemon juice, salt and olive oil in a food processor and process until smooth. Add water (about ½ cup) to thin hummus to the desired consistency. Transfer to a serving bowl and drizzle with additional olive oil to keep the hummus from crusting. Add garnish. Refrigerate until ready to use.

Serve with pita chips or fresh vegetables for dipping.

Yield: 4 cups

·9·

Kansas Dirt

—— and ——

Campus Cuisine

Recipes

Dining Rooms off Campus

"Our cook, Nordy, loved the Chi O's and we loved her," wrote Nancy Giesch Ingram. This salad was a favorite at the Chi Omega house in the 1970s, when there were fraternity houseboys and cooks parades. To say thank you for another great meal, the coeds sang a special song to the tune of "The Farmer in the Dell."

"Pleasing a sorority house full of women couldn't have been easy, but I will always remember sisters congregating in the kitchen…just like we did at home, watching Nordy (Nordstrom) prepare her specials and hearing her advice, which was freely given!" Ingram added.

NORDY'S K-STATE SALAD SPECIAL ✤✤
From the Chi Omega House (c. 1970)

---

1 (10-ounce) package fresh
    spinach
8 ounces fresh bean sprouts
1 (6-ounce) can water
    chestnuts, sliced and
    drained
4 hard cooked eggs, cut in
    slices or large dices
6 strips bacon, cooked crisp
    and crumbled

DRESSING:
1 cup oil
½ cup white vinegar
¾ cup sugar
¼ cup brown sugar, packed
⅓ cup catsup
1 tablespoon Worcestershire
    sauce
1 medium onion, chopped

Wash, dry and remove stems from spinach. Tear into pieces. Add sprouts, water chestnuts, eggs and bacon. Toss gently.

Mix dressing ingredients and add desired amount to salad. Toss together.

YIELD: 6 TO 8 SERVINGS

Every Day Is Kansas Dirt Day

Two recipes stand out in all the conversations, requests and submissions collected for *Teatime to Tailgates*. One of them is K-State Crowns (bread) and the other is this one, Kansas Dirt. "I love this recipe because it truly represents what Kansas is for me," said Valerie Tan, a native of Malaysia who graduated in 2009.

Graduate Julie Midgley lived in West Hall during the 2003–04 school year. She sends a love letter:

It was at the Derby Dining Center a couple months into the fall semester that my roommate and I and our friends discovered Kansas Dirt…served in generous squares to freshmen craving sugar and comfort. We waited for Kansas Dirt Day like small children wait for Christmas, searched the menus like they were Toys 'R Us catalogs. Then the day would arrive. When the Derb opened for dinner we descended all 5 flights of stairs like swift gazelles or perhaps stampeding buffalo. We're lucky no one was run over.

Bypassing long lines of sit-downers who inexplicably needed other food on Kansas Dirt Day, we chose Dashers, the to-go dining room. Low possibility of detection/judgment and whole trays of Dirt laid out for our enjoyment. How many servings could one fit in those Styrofoam leftover food containers, you ask? Four to six, seven if you really tried. Exhilarated, we returned to our rooms and feasted on nothing but Kansas Dirt and glasses of milk for the next few breakfasts, lunches and dinners.

Gluttonous? Yes. Shame? Absolutely none.

She adds: "Happy Anniversary K-State, and thank you to the Derb for the dessert and the great memories. Kansas Dirt is a perennial favorite in campus dining halls."

Today, Kansas Dirt is seldom off the menu on campus.

KANSAS DIRT ✤✤

From K-State Housing and Dining Services

1 (20-ounce) package chocolate sandwich cookies such as Oreos	1 cup powdered sugar
	1 teaspoon vanilla
	3 cups milk
8 ounces cream cheese, softened	2 (3½-ounce) packages vanilla instant pudding
½ cup butter, softened	12 ounces whipped topping

In a sealable bag or food processor, crush cookies. Measure half the crumbs into a 9 x 13-inch pan and press into bottom of the pan.

Beat cream cheese until smooth. Add butter, powdered sugar and vanilla and beat on medium speed with an electric mixture for one minute. In a separate bowl, beat pudding with milk as directed on pudding package. Gently combine the cream cheese mixture with the pudding. Fold in whipped topping.

Spread on top of the crumbs then sprinkle remaining crumbs over the top of the pudding. Refrigerate until firm.

YIELD: 12 SERVINGS

OPTIONAL SERVING SUGGESTIONS: The dirt can be frozen. Or assemble in small flower pot-shaped containers and decorate with gummy worm candy.

Merna Zeigler's Legacy

The K-State Union Food Service fed many students who lived off-campus. Townspeople regularly dined there in the evenings and for Sunday dinner. "Merna Zeigler was very good. She was one of the reasons we went to the Union to eat," remembered Nancy Prawl who worked on the histories of the Domestic Science and the Social Club. "Each table had a bread 'crown' and Merna would bring around plastic bags so people could take home the leftovers," Mrs. Prawl said.

Mrs. Zeigler graduated from K-State with a BS in 1932 and a MS in 1945. She was food service director at the K-State Union for more than 20 years and retired in the mid-1970s as associate professor emeritus in dietetics and restaurant and institutional management.

Bernice E. Kelly, who now lives in New Zealand, was a graduate student in food service administration when she worked with Merna Zeigler in 1965 and 1966. "The highlight for me and most popular function was the Swedish Smorgasbord served on 2 consecutive days, 2 sittings per day, in late

Under the direction of Merna Zeigler, associate professor and food service director, the K-State Student Union served elaborate holiday and international dinners to the community. This undated photo is from a homecoming buffet. Courtesy of Morse Department of Special Collections, Kansas State University Libraries

November…approximately 25 different products required very good planning and cooperation between the kitchen on the ground floor and the banquet hall on the floor above," she says.

Diners called the bread Crown Rolls but Mrs. Zeigler always corrected them. They were K-State Crowns. The signature bread of Kansas State University has been served to faculty, students, staff, dignitaries and other guests for several generations.

Here is Mrs. Zeigler's recipe adapted by Camilla Korenek for a bread machine. Korenek is an instructor in hospitality management and dietetics and directs dining services at Van Zile Hall.

MERNA ZEIGLER'S K-STATE CROWN ✤✤

1½ cups lukewarm water
(100–115°F)
¾ cup lukewarm milk (95°F,
warm 35 seconds in high-
powered microwave)
1 egg
3½ cups bread flour
3 tablespoons sugar
3 tablespoons vegetable
shortening or butter

1½ teaspoons salt
2 (.025-ounce) packages active
dry yeast
¼ cup pecan pieces
¾ cup granulated sugar
1 teaspoon cinnamon
3–4 tablespoons melted butter
5–7 whole maraschino cherries
Pecans halves

Load water, milk and egg into bread machine. Add flour, sugar, butter and salt. Top with yeast.

Set bread cycle to dough. Remove dough from machine upon completion of the cycle.

Preheat oven to 350°F. Grease with shortening or coat the bottom and sides of a tube cake pan with nonstick cooking spray.

Sprinkle pecan pieces in bottom of pan. Mix together ¾ cup sugar and cinnamon. Divide dough into 18 equal pieces. Form each piece into a uniform roll. Lightly coat each roll with oil and roll in cinnamon-sugar mixture. Arrange twelve rolls on the outside and six rolls in the middle of the pan. Cover; let rise until double.

Bake for 40 minutes or until done. Tent top with foil if necessary to prevent over-browning.

YIELD: 18 SERVINGS

❖❖ MERNA ZEIGLER'S HOT CHICKEN SALAD

2 cups diced cooked chicken	Salt
1½ cups diced celery	Pepper
¼ cup chopped almonds	⅔ cup mayonnaise
2 teaspoons chopped onion	1 cup grated cheddar cheese
1 teaspoon grated lemon zest	1 cup broken potato chips
1 tablespoon lemon juice	

Preheat oven to 375°F. Butter a 1½-quart casserole.

Mix chicken, celery, almonds, onion, zest, lemon juice, salt and pepper to taste. Add mayonnaise. Transfer to prepared dish.

Toss together cheese and potato chips. Distribute atop chicken mixture. Bake for 20 to 30 minutes.

YIELD: 4 SERVINGS

I retrieved this recipe from my battered metal recipe box in the basement. I collected it when I was a student in the 1960s to use in a meal preparation class perhaps, and then forgot about it. Since I asked others to walk down memory lane, I did too. I loved this dish and, when I made it again in the 21st century, it still tickles my fancy. I use chicken thighs but any pieces will work. Adjust cooking time accordingly.

ORIENTAL CHERRY CHICKEN ✤ ✤

From K-State University's Student Union (c. 1967)

2½ to 3 pounds chicken pieces	1 (14.5-ounce) can tart red cherries
½ cup flour	1 tablespoon flour
1 teaspoon salt	½ cup sugar
1 teaspoon pepper	1 orange, thinly sliced (unpeeled)
¼ cup butter	½ cup toasted almonds, slivered
¼ cup lard or shortening	

Mix ½ cup flour, salt and pepper. Dredge chicken pieces in the mixture, shaking off all excess flour. In large heavy skillet, heat butter and lard. When hot, fry chicken for about 10 minutes on each side or until done. Meat or juice should not be pink.

Remove chicken from pan and set aside. Remove all but ⅓ cup drippings from the frying pan. Drain cherries; reserve juice. Combine 1 tablespoon flour and reserved juice, stirring until flour is dissolved.

Heat drippings in pan and add cherries and sugar until boiling, stir juice into cherry mixture and cook until thick and clear. Add chicken. Cover pan and cook for 5 minutes. Turn chicken, stirring sauce to make sure the caramelized portions do not scorch. Add orange and almonds. Cover and heat for 5 more minutes.

Serve with rice. Garnish with additional orange slices if desired.

YIELD: 4 SERVINGS

In the Creative Cafeteria Line

If there was an Academy Award for campus cuisine, K-State's residence hall food would win perpetually. Dining services and its dietitians have carried off most of the major accolades in the field. They feed more than 5,000 students each year in nine residence halls, one leadership/scholarship house and the Jardine apartment community.

Its history, so closely linked with what is now the College of Human Ecology, began more than a century ago when professors and cooking class students were put in charge of feeding the campus. In 1877 the classes put their new knowledge to work by serving lunches and dinners to faculty and students for 10 cents a meal.

One student told this story, recorded by Ruth Hoeflin in *History of a College*: "Economy in the weekly meals served to the faculty in Anderson Hall was stressed to extent that each week the same lettuce leaves were carefully washed and used again. At that time the Emily Post of the day did not believe it proper to eat one's lettuce. The plan worked fine until the day Professor Willard, a faculty guest, ate his lettuce. This meant there wasn't enough for the following week—very upsetting to the budget."

In 1915, the college asked Margaret Haggard to teach students how to direct cafeterias. She became associate professor of domestic science (later called the Department of Institutional Economics and today Hospitality Management and Dietetics) and director of the cafeteria and tea room in Kedzie Hall.

Starting in 1898 in the basement of Kedzie Hall, domestic science students learned quantity food preparation and served lunch to other students for 10 cents, undated. Courtesy of Morse Department of Special Collections, Kansas State University Libraries

BETTIE GARRISON AND HER TRUNK ARRIVED IN 1938

Bettie Garrison Ore, Paola, graduated in 1942 with a degree in home economics. She wrote this story about life in Van Zile Hall, years she calls "unforgettable, exciting, frustrating and, most of all, wonderful."

In September of 1938 my trunk and I were deposited outside the doorway of Van Zile Hall in Manhattan. It was the way most students arrived at Kansas State Agricultural College in 1938. To a timid and shy student, the building seemed large indeed. I had just come from a small rural town of about 500 people to a place where there were six times that many in the college alone. Van Zile was the largest girls' dormitory on the campus and most of the girls who were not in sororities lived there. It was just at the close of the Great Depression and was a more affordable place to live. They offered two plans to pay for room and board. For $30 a month you received a room and three meals a day. The other, most used, allowed a student to work around 10 hours per week for three weeks and gave you the fourth one off. The work consisted of light housekeeping duties, work in the kitchen and some limited desk duty. Life was comparatively easy. A house mother looked after our general behavior, welfare and, above all, manners. We were allowed to be casual at breakfast - pajamas and hair in curlers. Lunch was school dress; it was a more organized meal. As for dinner, we would not have to dress up, but our hair had to be combed and a general proper appearance presented. Sunday was dress-up day, hose and heels, good clothes, white tablecloths and linen napkins. We had our own napkin rings which were put in place at dinner. The tables seated six; each table had one person directing the serving and ending the meal. After Sunday's meal, the time was spent singing sorority, fraternity and college songs. It was a grand and pleasant memory. We were always told that Van Zile had the best meals on campus. No doubt this was true, because the dietetic students were required to spend one semester their senior year interning in the kitchen under the supervision of Miss Lavalle Wood. Her job (privilege) was to turn naïve, unskilled students into first class dietitians. She did it by skill, by intimidation, and by caring. Her students went out in to the world as some of the best prepared in the country. Most girls were terrified when they first met her. She reduced many of them to tears in the beginning, but by the time they graduated, their admiration was endless. As for food that was served, my memory is a bit cloudy after 70 years. We all came from humble homes in rural Kansas where our mothers were competent cooks who often struggled to have enough on the table, regardless of how it was served! At Van Zile, we had foods many of us had never seen or eaten before. Many pounds were gained that first year. Only two of those foods stay in my memory. Being served sherbet as a salad with a main course was different. It was elegant. The other was a dessert, simple but impressive. On a small white plate was a cone of powdered sugar surrounded by fat, very ripe strawberries with their stems. I thought it was the fanciest of fancy.

The number of diners soon swamped the space and Thompson Hall was built in 1922. The cafeteria and Open Door Tea Room served students and faculty members every day and housed special parties and dinners for college groups. A 24-cent luncheonette included salad, meat, bread, butter and beverage.

When the K-State Union was completed in 1955, food service moved there.

Van Zile Hall, built in 1926, had its own dining room, or as Roger Townley calls it, "the beloved dining hall." "I have fond memories of the Kansas Day dinners and Valentine's Day meals with candlelight and special cake," he said of his student years in the early 1970s.

Van Zile was an honors dorm then and didn't serve breakfast. The young men walked to Putnam or Boyd and ate with the coeds. Townley told this story: "The women would wear PJs and curlers to breakfast and we didn't like that. So a bunch of guys decided they would dress that way. We got curlers and robes and we made sure they paid attention to us. And we made our statement.

"Our 'private' dining room was closed on the weekends so we had to slum it at Derby. We loved going to the Gold Room on Sundays after church...We had to look legit, not wear a coat and cutoffs," he adds. "It was the elite place to eat on campus"

The 1975 graduate in bakery science and management wasn't the only one to recall "the creations of generations of K-Staters who were forced to make their own meals on Sunday nights. I'm surprised nobody ever burned down their dorm attempting to use their popcorn popper like a hibachi grill."

Gloria Freeland, a graduate who now teaches journalism at K-State, recalls Sunday fondue parties spread on her dorm room floor.

Townley, who lived for two years in Straube Scholarship House, filled with its own food traditions and stories, came from a K-State family. Dad, three brothers, two sisters-in-law and his wife Jane are all K-State graduates. Today he heads Townley Associates, based in North Carolina, that consults on food product development and related technical services. He still recalls the homemade salad dressings, especially this one. Until the 1980s, dining services made all its dressings.

TOMATO SOUP SALAD DRESSING ✦ ✦

From K-State Dining Services

5 tablespoons sugar

1 teaspoon salt

½ teaspoon dry mustard

½ teaspoon paprika

1 cup plus 1 tablespoon
concentrated tomato soup

3 tablespoons vinegar

½ cup salad oil

1 small clove garlic, minced

Combine sugar, salt, mustard, paprika and canned soup. Add vinegar, oil and garlic and mix until well blended. Refrigerate.

YIELD: ABOUT 1 CUP

Many community cookbooks from the 1960s and '70s printed recipes for Russian Cream. This one was a favorite in the 1970s in the K-State dining halls.

RUSSIAN CREAM ✦ ✦

From K-State Dining Services

¾ cup half and half

½ cup sugar

1½ teaspoons gelatin

6 tablespoons cold water

¾ cup sour cream

½ teaspoon vanilla

Red raspberries

Combine half and half with sugar. Heat to 185°F. Sprinkle gelatin in cold water. Do not stir. Let stand 5 minutes then add to hot cream. Stir to dissolve. Cool.

Transfer to a mixer bowl. Add sour cream and mix thoroughly. Stir in vanilla. Spoon into dessert dishes. Chill. Garnish with red raspberries.

YIELD: 8 SERVINGS

No, Grandma Didn't Invent this Cake

When I was a kid, I thought my grandmother invented this cake in her Chase County farm kitchen. Grandma Flora Pretzer, the dessert baking queen, taught me a vital life lesson: pie and cake are breakfast foods.

But she didn't invent it. Food historian Jean Anderson called this one of the most popular recipes of the 20th century. The recipe dates back to the 1950s. Some people call it Texas Sheet Cake or Sheath Cake or credit a family member. Some use sour cream instead of buttermilk.

Many K-State graduates call it Boyd Hall Brownies. Suzanne Carlson found this recipe in her battered copy of the 75-page *Favorite Recipes of Boyd Hall, Spring 1973.* The book has a list of food service people like "Boyd's salad lady."

The Kansas Wheat Commission adapted a healthier version from a recipe first printed in 1988 in the *National School Food Service and Nutrition Magazine.* Theirs called for whole wheat flour, half the amount of sugar and less butter or oil.

We will stick with the Boyd Hall recipe. Mrs. Carlson suggests topping with chopped nuts. Try Kansas black walnuts instead of the traditional pecans. Kansas grows more black walnuts than any other state.

BOYD HALL BUTTERMILK BROWNIES ✤ ✤

From Suzanne Carlson

½ cup margarine
½ cup shortening
1 cup water
¼ cup cocoa
2 cups flour
2 cups sugar

½ teaspoon salt
½ cup buttermilk
2 eggs
1 teaspoon soda
1 teaspoon vanilla
1 recipe frosting (below)

Preheat oven to 350°F. Grease and flour a 11 x 16 x 2-inch jelly roll pan.

Heat margarine, shortening, water and cocoa until margarine melts. Add flour, sugar and salt and mix well. Blend in buttermilk, eggs, soda and vanilla. Mix and pour into prepared pan.

Bake for 30 minutes.

When done, remove from oven and frost immediately.

FROSTING:

½ cup margarine
¼ cup cocoa
⅓ cup buttermilk

4 cups powdered sugar
1 teaspoon vanilla
Pinch of salt

In a medium saucepan, bring margarine, cocoa and buttermilk to a boil. Remove from heat and add sugar, vanilla and salt. Blend completely. Nuts may be added on top.

YIELD: 12 SERVINGS

T*H*E Bakery

Birthday cake for your roomie? A Monster Cookie in the middle of the night? A peanut butter Rice Krispie Treat to treat yourself for finishing that paper? At The Bakery in Derby Dining Hall students grab and run back to the books, or buy and just hang out. It's a place where K-State memories are made, and many of those memories involve Monster Cookies and Chocolate Cappuccino Crumb Muffins.

Monster Cookies are the all-time favorite at The Bakery and at the athletic training table. (Recipe on page 42)

The CornerStone Coffee and Bakery, next door to the full-service restaurant named JP's at Jardine Marketplace, opened in 2011. The Bakery in Derby Dining Center is also a project of the K-State Housing and Dining Services. Courtesy of David Mayes, Kansas State University Division of Communications and Marketing.

CHOCOLATE CAPPUCCINO CRUMB MUFFINS ✦✦

From The Bakery in Derby Dining Center

1 cup plus 2 tablespoons whole milk
½ cup butter, melted
1 egg, slightly beaten
1 teaspoon vanilla
2 cups plus 3 tablespoons flour
½ cup plus 1 tablespoon sugar
¼ cup brown sugar
1 tablespoon baking powder
2 teaspoons instant coffee powder
¼ teaspoon salt

1 teaspoon cinnamon
¾ cup mini chocolate chips
1 cup chocolate chunks or
    regular chocolate chips

CRUMBLE:

4½ tablespoons butter, very cold
7 tablespoons flour
¼ cup brown sugar
½ teaspoon cinnamon

Preheat oven to 400°F.

Combine milk, butter, egg and vanilla in a small bowl. Set aside.

In a mixer bowl, blend flour, sugar, brown sugar, baking powder, coffee powder, salt and cinnamon. Add milk mixture all at once. Mix on low speed just to blend. Do not over mix.

Fold in chocolate chips and chunks and portion into paper-lined muffin tins. Fill tins half to ⅔ full.

Cut cold butter into chunks. With a mixer or fork, mix in 7 tablespoons flour, ¼ cup brown sugar and ½ teaspoon cinnamon. Mix until crumbly. Sprinkle over muffins.

Bake for about 20 minutes.

YIELD: 18 MUFFINS

In Clovia's Kitchen

Clovia House got its unofficial start in 1930 when several coeds with 4-H backgrounds envisioned a house where they could live and work together. Sororities were expensive; dormitories were nonexistent. With support from the state home economics leader and from cafeteria director Bessie West, they found a house and recruited students for the cooperative living experiment. In 1932 the students selected a name, Clovia after the 4-H symbol, and wrote bylaws and became official.

Nancy Rezac, a 1971 graduate who lives in St. Marys, asked her Clovia House sisters to help compile food memories. Their stories illustrate that there is more to kitchens than food.

Nina Felbush Seibert, Class of 1968: "In the spring of 1967 I had cooking duty with the late Marlyse Milburn. We were to fix pizza for supper. We really wanted to do pepperoni but we didn't have any so we tried to spice up hotdogs. Needless to say the pizza left much to be desired."

Cassandra Mikel Elsworth, Class of 1983: "Oh my goodness, do you remember Eggs a la Goldenrod? I certainly do! YUCK."

DeAnn Hauser, Class of 1981: "One memory that comes to mind is the number of in depth conversations shared in the kitchen at the end of the day. A good place to vent about grades and boys. Also a chance to talk about future hopes and dreams."

Jeannie Warren Lindsay, Class of 1951: "'This isn't a boarding house!' exclaimed Ginny Grandfield, Clovia president, 1947-48. Another girl and I were serving fruit in sauce dishes as dessert on a Saturday night—and we weren't putting plates under those sauce dishes. We got the plates quickly—and to this day, I can't serve food in sauce dishes without a plate underneath, thanks to Ginny, my idol that year."

Margaret Arwood Hickson, Class of 1954: "Snickerdoodles for breakfast."

Mildred (Millie) Hundley Horlacher, Class of 1953: "My Clovia cookbook is in a Ziplock bag to save its well-used pages. Meals were special times. The kitchen was a wonderful place even though it did not have the latest appliances… The friendships made there have continued through the decades."

Many lauded Clovia House Rolls, but the favorite of Julie A. Sellers, who works as a federally certified court interpreter, is Clovia Coffee Cake. "Living at the Alpha of Clovia 4-H Scholarship house at KSU was a family tradition that began with my Aunt Betty in the 1950s. My older female cousins and my older sister all lived at Clovia, so there was no doubt in my mind that I wanted to live there as well. My family had been making the famous Clovia Coffee Cake for years, so I already felt like I was part of the sisterhood."

CLOVIA COFFEE CAKE ❖❖

From Pauline Wood Ferrell
Published in Our Favorite Recipes *(c. 1972)*

3 cups flour	1 teaspoon vanilla
3 teaspoons baking powder	1 cup milk
½ teaspoons salt	1 cup brown sugar
1 cup oil	1 teaspoon cinnamon
1 cup sugar	½ to 1 cup chopped pecans
2 eggs	½ cup melted margarine

Preheat oven to 350°F. Grease and flour a 9 x 13-inch baking pan.

Sift together flour, baking powder and salt and set aside.

In large bowl, combine oil, sugar, eggs and vanilla. Cream until blended well. Add dry ingredients alternately with milk, stirring after each addition.

In a separate bowl, mix together brown sugar, cinnamon and pecans.

Pour half of batter into prepared pan. Top with half the sugar mixture. Repeat layers. Pour melted margarine over top. Bake for 35 minutes or until done.

YIELD: 12 SERVINGS

·10·

A Community
—— *of* ——
Cooks

Recipes

IN HER BOOK *Eat My Words: Reading Women's Lives through the Cookbooks They Wrote*, Janet Theophano wrote about cookbooks as communities, as collective memory and identity, as legacy and as autobiography.

The first cookbook ever produced by K–State faculty, staff or students and possibly the oldest community-based cookbook in Manhattan, *Kansas Kook-Book for Kansas Kooks*, was published in 1900. It was compiled by graduates and students of KSAC and edited by Myrtle Mather, Elizabeth J. Agnew, Mary Bly Pritner and Mary Waugh. A note in the pages indicates "recipes are edited from lectures and lessons given in class work, by Prof Minnie A. Stoner."

The recipes are printed here just as they appear in Hale Library's well-worn copy of the small paper-cover book. These two were not from class but from past professor Nellie Sawyer Kedzie, who was then teaching at Brandley Polytechnic Institute, and from Lydia G. Willard, wife of chemistry professor Julius T. Willard, born near Wabaunsee in 1862, and educated at KSAC. In 1940, Julius Willard published a comprehensive detailed history of the college and was listed as the college historian.

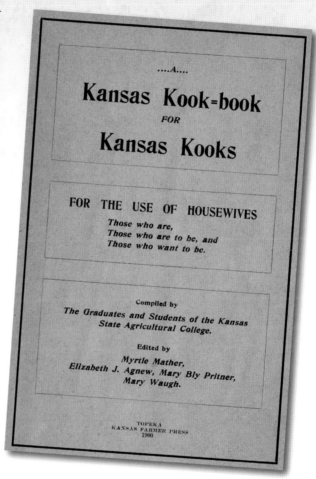

....A....

Kansas Kook=book

FOR

Kansas Kooks

FOR THE USE OF HOUSEWIVES

Those who are,
Those who are to be, and
Those who want to be.

Compiled by
The Graduates and Students of the Kansas
State Agricultural College.

Edited by
Myrtle Mather,
Elizabeth J. Agnew, Mary Bly Pritner,
Mary Waugh.

TOPEKA
KANSAS FARMER PRESS
1900

The title page of Kansas Kook-Book for Kansas Kooks *published by K-State students in 1900.* COURTESY OF MORSE DEPARTMENT OF SPECIAL COLLECTIONS, KANSAS STATE UNIVERSITY LIBRARIES

✥✥ PRUNE SOUFFLÉ

From Nellie Sawyer Kedzie (1900)

Soak 1 lb. prunes 24 hrs. Cook slowly until soft. Rub through coarse sieve and add 1 c. sugar and 1 tsp. vanilla. Fold into stiffly beaten whites of 6 eggs and bake in buttered pan for 1 hr. Best while warm with whipped cream.

✥✥ NUT SALAD

From Lydia Gardiner Willard (1900)

2 lbs. English walnuts (before the shell is removed), 4 medium sized bunches of celery, 1 c. mayonnaise dressing, 1 c. rich sweet cream.

Cut nut kernels with a knife into pieces about the size of peas. Cut the celery into fine bits, whip the cream and blend it with the mayonnaise dressing. Chill all of the ingredients. Just before serving mix the nuts and celery and marinate with dressing. This quantity will serve 15 people.

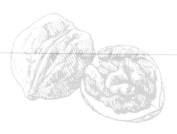

A Community of Recipes

Over 150 years, K-State groups published a number of community-style cookbooks that have raised money for the library, the alumni association, scholarships and more. Among them are:

- *Cats in the Kitchen* (2009). Not surprisingly, editors Dena Bunnel, Lauren Luhrs and Matt Wagner included offerings such as Chari Lacey Miller's Break 'em Hawk Bites that calls for "Hawk Breasts" or boneless, skinless, chicken breasts. She recommended they be served before the annual KSU vs. KU football game.

- Three creative offerings by the library: *Festive Foods from Farrell* (1980), *KSU Libraries Staff Association Cookbook* (1999) and *Reader's Digestion, A K-State Libraries Cookbook* (2005).

- *Note-able Cooks* (c. 1976). A project of the Music Service Guild of KSU compiled by Dorothy Rehschuh, it is more fun than tubas at a pep rally. Creative solicitation yielded recipes from celebrities, government officials, campus hot shots and people like Ronna Rounds from White Horse, Yukon, who contributed a recipe entitled "How to braise moose meat." Instructions start out: "Take a walk in the snowy country. Sight moose. Shoot same. Skin, butcher, pack meat and tote back to cabin in the country."

- *KSU Dames Favorite Recipes* (1975). The club was made up of married women students and married students' wives.

- *Kids in the Kitchen* (1987). From KSU Child Care Cooperative and Kansas Home Economics Association.

- *How to Cook a Wildcat* (2006). A project of Student Dietetic Association.

- *K-Taste!* (2006). K-State Housings & Dining Services Recipe Collection.

- *Food for Five* (1984). Janet Helm, a graduate research assistant then, put this gem together with help from her fellow students, faculty, alumni and friends of the Department of Dietetics, Restaurant and Institutional Management to raise money for the annual Grace M. Shugart lecture. They coined the name from *Food for Fifty*.

❖❖ ARTICHOKE DIP

From Amy Button Renz
Published in Cats in the Kitchen
Served at the dedication of the K-State Alumni Center in 2002

1 (14-ounce) can artichoke hearts, drained	1 cup freshly-grated parmesan cheese
	1 cup mayonnaise

Chop artichoke hearts. Mix with cheese and mayonnaise and spread into 8 or 9-inch pie pan. Bake for 25 minutes. Serve hot with pita chips.

YIELD: 2 CUPS

❖❖ SUNFLOWER CANDY

From Orlain Ambrose
Published in Note-able Cooks

¼ cup butter	½ teaspoon vanilla
1 cup sugar	1 cup unsalted sunflower seeds, toasted in oven
Dash salt	
½ cup white corn syrup	

Boil butter, sugar, salt and syrup until hard crack stage (300–310°F on candy thermometer). Add vanilla and seeds. Pour into buttered cookie sheet. It should be very thin. When cool, break into pieces.

YIELD: ABOUT 2 CUPS

WHEAT BERRY SALAD ✤ ✤

From Erin Flock Laurie
Published in Cats in the Kitchen
Celebrates the Wheat State

2 cups dried wheat berries	4 stalks celery, diced
¼ cup extra virgin olive oil	1 red pepper, diced
2 tablespoons balsamic vinegar	⅔ cup crumbled feta cheese
⅛ teaspoon freshly ground pepper	½ cup sliced black olives
	½ cup chopped parsley
¼ teaspoon salt	¼ cup chopped cilantro

Soak wheat berries in water for 8 hours or overnight. Rinse and place in large sauce pan with 4 cups of water. Bring to a boil. Reduce heat to simmer and cook berries 1 hour or until the grains are plump and a few have burst. Remove from heat and drain any excess liquid. Chill berries. To make dressing, whisk together olive oil, vinegar, pepper and salt in a bowl. Set aside.

To prepare salad, place grain in large bowl. Add celery, red pepper, cheese, olives, parsley and cilantro. Stir with dressing until well blended.

Chill for at least 30 minutes before serving.

YIELD: 8 SERVINGS

Describing farm belt cooking in 1952, Nell Nichols wrote about women with "meat-potato-gravy husbands" and their interpretations of salads. She paid special attention to tomatoes, cabbage, wilted lettuce and molded salads. "Although Kansas and Nebraska hostesses seldom realize it, one of their A-1 fruit salads is gelatinized by the marshmallows it contains. They make this treat year in and year out for special occasions," she continued.

The salad, which became popular in the 1930s, has several monikers: Overnight Fruit Salad, 24-Hour Salad, Millionaire Salad, Marshmallow Salad and Forgotten Salad. A distant cousin is Frog Eye Salad using acini di pepe pasta.

✤✤ 24-HOUR SALAD

From Mrs. Duane Lowdon, Cawker City
Published in Note-able Cooks

3 beaten egg yolks	1 cup mandarin oranges,
2 tablespoons sugar	drained
2 tablespoons lemon juice	1 cup pecan halves
2 tablespoons pineapple juice	2 cups white grapes
⅛ teaspoon salt	2 cups pineapple tidbits,
1 tablespoon butter	drained
1 cup whipped cream	1 cup maraschino cherries,
2 cups miniature marshmallows	drained

Cook egg yolks, sugar, lemon juice, pineapple juice, salt and butter until thick and cool thoroughly. Add whipped cream and fold in marshmallows, oranges, pecans, grapes, pineapple and cherries. Chill at least 24 hours.

Yield: 10 servings

WATERMELON ICE ✢ ✢

From Jennifer and Jamie Kendall
Published in Kids in the Kitchen *(1987)*

4–6 cups seeded watermelon   1 tablespoon sugar (optional)
1 tablespoon lemon juice   1½ cups crushed ice

Put watermelon, lemon and sugar in blender and blend thoroughly. Add ice and blend at high speed. Pour in glasses and serve.

YIELD: 6 SERVINGS

VARNISHED BACON ✢ ✢

From Allene G. Vaden
Published in Food for Five *(1984)*

---

1 pound thick bacon, slices   1 pound brown sugar
cut into thirds   3 tablespoons flour

Mix sugar and flour. Pat mixture on both sides of bacon and place on foil-lined baking pan. Bake for 10 minutes, remove immediately. Drain on brown paper.

YIELD: 6 TO 8 SERVINGS

Friends and Family, Recipes and Memories

This recipe comes from Darline Conover's recipe box. Robert Conover was editor of *Kansas Magazine* and on the faculty of the English department. He retired in the early 1950s. Both the Conovers graduated from K-State as did their children Robert Jr. and Liz. Clementine Paddleford wrote about Mrs. Conover's cooking in one of her national newspaper columns.

❖❖ GINGERBREAD WAFFLES
From Darline Conover (c. 1978)

2 eggs

¼ cup sugar

½ cup molasses

1 cup sour milk (or 1
   cup milk mixed with
   1 teaspoon vinegar)

1½ cups flour

1 teaspoon ground ginger

¼ teaspoon salt

1 teaspoon baking powder

6 tablespoons melted fat/
   butter/margarine

Beat eggs until light; add sugar, molasses and sour milk. Sift together flour, ginger, salt and baking powder. Add to egg mixture. Beat until smooth, add fat and stir. Bake in waffle iron.

YIELD: 4 TO 5 WAFFLES

Politics and Chocolate Cake

Mary Ellen Hull McCaffree ran for office in Washington State because her children's schools were overcrowded and underfunded. She was a "relentless taker-on-of-tasks," had been since her days as a home economics student at K-State. She graduated from K-State in 1941 and her mother, Mary Alberta Johnson, graduated in 1914 or 1915.

The homemaker and mother of five stumped for a job in the state legislature, was elected and stayed in office from 1962 to 1970. She was the first woman director of the Washington State Department of Revenue and an unrelenting voice encouraging women to take active roles in politics.

McCaffree wrote about her experiences in *Politics of the Possible, The Decade Our American Democracy Worked*. A campaign handout card read, "And here's another good recipe. Re-elect Mary Ellen McCaffree." The card included this recipe. The cake gets its upside down name because as it bakes, a rich pudding forms at the bottom and the cake rises to the top.

CHOCOLATE UPSIDE DOWN CAKE ✤ ✤

From Mary Ellen Hull McCaffree

---

1 cup flour	1 teaspoon vanilla
¾ cup sugar	½ cup nuts, chopped
2 tablespoons cocoa	
2 teaspoons baking powder	TOPPING:
¼ teaspoon salt	½ cup white sugar
½ cup milk	½ cup brown sugar
2 tablespoons butter, melted	2 tablespoons cocoa

Preheat oven to 350°F. Butter and flour an 8 x 8-inch cake pan.

Mix together flour, sugar, cocoa, baking powder and salt. Add milk, butter, vanilla and nuts and blend. Pour into prepared pan. Mix the three topping ingredients thoroughly and sprinkle over batter. Pour 1 cup cold water over the top.

Bake 30 minutes. Leave it in the pan until ready to serve.

YIELD: 6 SERVINGS

An Emphasis on Health

Ron Ibbetson got a BS degree in dairy production and a MS degree in agronomy and was a member of the dairy, dairy products and crop judging teams at K-State. Clara Jane Holloway Ibbetson had an assistantship in foods and nutrition.

After K-State, work took them to Colby where she taught nutrition and he was a soils fertility specialist at the experiment station. From there they moved to Arizona where she was a nutritionist for the Yuma County WIC program and he was an agronomist for Sakata Seed Company, developing broccoli and other vegetable seeds.

These are a couple of her family's favorite recipes from Mrs. Ibbetson's *Smart Eating Made Simple*, a book about healthy eating with whole grains and fresh vegetables. She serves the chili sauce with vegetables.

❖❖ SWEET CHILI SAUCE

From Jane Ibbetson

1½ teaspoons red chili flakes

2 cups maple syrup

3 tablespoons raw cider vinegar

4 tablespoons sherry or mirin

4 tablespoons tamari soy sauce

2 teaspoons ginger, grated

3 cloves garlic, smashed

¼ teaspoon paprika

½ teaspoon pepper

Combine all ingredients in a small saucepan. Simmer over low heat until thickened, about 30 minutes.

Store in refrigerator. Serve with vegetables, especially good with steamed Brussels sprouts, or use as a marinade for chicken.

YIELD: 2 CUPS

BROWN RICE PUDDING WITH HAZELNUT CREAM ✤ ✤

By Jane Ibbetson

2½ cups cooked brown rice

3 eggs, beaten

1½ cups unsweetened
    canned coconut milk

⅓ cup maple syrup

2 teaspoons vanilla

1 teaspoon cinnamon

½ teaspoon nutmeg

⅛ teaspoon sea salt

1 cup raisins

½ cup roasted walnuts or
    pecans, chopped

Preheat oven to 325°F.

Thoroughly combine all ingredients. Pour into a lightly greased 2-quart casserole dish. Bake for 50 to 55 minutes. Serve with Hazelnut Cream.

YIELD: 8 TO 10 SERVINGS

HAZELNUT CREAM

1 cup unsweetened canned
    coconut milk

¼ cup date syrup (available
    at Middle Eastern markets)

2 teaspoons hazelnut extract

½ teaspoon vanilla extract

Using an immersion blender, puree all ingredients. Store in a glass jar in the refrigerator. Allow to come to room temperature before serving on the pudding.

YIELD: 1½ CUPS

Here We Go A'Pumpkin Caroling

Charlie Brown started it. Karla Hughes and Amelia Brown were graduate students in foods and nutrition in the early 1970s when they bought "Pumpkin Carols," a booklet featuring *Peanuts* comic characters. Lucy, Charlie Brown and the gang were dressed up in Halloween costumes singing old favorites such as "Pumpkin bell, pumpkin bells…"

Why not organize the grad students, put on white lab coats and hair nets, carry pots and pans for percussion and carol at faculty homes on Halloween? "Being forewarned, most faculty invited us into their homes for gingerbread, cookies, popcorn balls, hot chocolate, and spiced cider. Pumpkin Caroling was a tradition thereafter," they said.

Gwen Tinklin, the department head, served these cookies at Pumpkin Caroling and other times when she thought her students deserved a little something extra.

❖❖ GWEN TINKLIN'S OATMEAL COOKIES

From Amelia Brown and Karla Hughes

1 cup brown sugar	**⅛ teaspoon salt**
1 cup white sugar	**1 teaspoon vanilla**
1 cup shortening or butter	**1 cup coconut**
2 eggs	**4 cups rolled oats**
1 cup flour	**1 cup nuts, chopped**
1 teaspoon soda	

Preheat oven to 350°F.

Cream together sugars and butter. Add eggs and beat well. Add flour, soda, salt, vanilla, coconut, oatmeal and nuts. Combine thoroughly.

Roll into balls the size of walnuts. Place on cookie sheets about 1 inch apart and bake for 10 to 12 minutes.

YIELD: ABOUT 4 DOZEN COOKIES

Reversing Directions: From Kitchen to Classroom

Joshua O'Neal had spent more than 16 years as a chef, including stints at two Arizona 4 Diamond restaurants, when he ran away with the pastry chef. Carmen O'Neal decided she wanted to dive deeper into the baking business; Joshua decided he'd spent enough time on his feet in a white chef's coat.

They moved from Scottsdale, Arizona, to Manhattan, Kansas, where she is enrolled in the bakery science and management program and he pursues a graduate degree in public health, working as a graduate assistant in the College of Education.

Textbooks and research replaced their kitchen careers. Today they take turns cooking at home; they dine better—and with more panache—than most.

In Arizona restaurants, Joshua O'Neal spent a lot of time around mole (MOH-lay), the spicy Mexican sauce that uses a small amount of Mexican chocolate. He uses this recipe on beef, pork, and, here, with lime grilled chicken.

"There is only one way to make mole, and that's the right way," the chef-graduate student says. "This recipe is involved! But it's worth it."

LIME GRILLED CHICKEN ✤✤

By Joshua O'Neal

---

6 small boneless skinless
   chicken breasts
1 lime, juiced
1 ounce tequila (optional)
1 tablespoon white vinegar
¼ cup water

⅓ cup olive oil
2 tablespoons fresh cilantro,
   chopped
1 teaspoon cumin powder
1 teaspoon salt
½ teaspoon black pepper

In a large bowl, whisk together lime juice, tequila, vinegar, water, oil, cilantro, cumin, salt and pepper. Add chicken and marinate in the refrigerator for 2 to 4 hours.

Cook chicken on hot grill for 12 to 15 minutes.

Serve plain or with mole.

YIELD: 6 SERVINGS

✤✤ MOLE WITH LIME GRILLED CHICKEN

By Joshua O'Neal

---

2 Ancho chilies, de-stemmed
    and deseeded (retain seeds
    in a small saucepan for roasting)
½ ounce sliced almonds
1 teaspoon peppercorns, cracked
1 Guajillo chili, de-stemmed
    and deseeded (discard seeds)
3 New Mexican chilies,
    de-stemmed and deseeded
    (discard seeds)
½ cup plus 2–3 teaspoons
    vegetable oil, divided
2 cloves garlic, peeled and
    smashed

½ medium onion, chopped
1½ tablespoons raisins
½ stick cinnamon (cracked)
½ pound roma tomatoes, halved
1 slice white bread
1 (12-inch) flour tortilla
¾ tablet Ibarra Mexican chocolate
1 tablespoon chicken stock
1 teaspoon salt
½ cup sugar
Lime Grilled Chicken
    (recipe previous page)
½ cup cojita cheese

Begin boiling 1¼ quarts of water in a large saucepan.

To a small saucepan, add ancho seeds, almonds and peppercorns. Toast over medium heat (no oil) and cool.

In a separate skillet, toast chilies in 2 teaspoons vegetable oil over medium heat for about 5 minutes. Add garlic, onion, raisins, cinnamon stick and cut tomatoes. Cook for 2 additional minutes on low heat. If too dry, add another teaspoon of oil.

After the chilies, garlic, raisins, cinnamon, tomatoes and onions have been cooked, add them to the boiling water. Add bread and tortilla.

Next, add the seed mixture, vegetable oil, chocolate, stock and salt to the boiling water. Let simmer approximately 30 minutes. Remove from heat and cool to about 110°F. Remove cinnamon stick.

After cooling, puree in blender in batches. Do not blend while hot. Do blend until smooth. After blended, return puree to stove in pan. Turn heat on low and add the sugar. Simmer uncovered until thick, about 20 minutes.

Pour mole over grilled chicken. Sprinkle with desired amount of cojita cheese.

YIELD: 12 SERVINGS

VENISON GYROS WITH TZATZIKI SAUCE ✦✦

By Joshua O'Neal

2 tablespoons olive oil

1½ tablespoons ground cumin

1 tablespoon minced garlic

1 tablespoon minced shallots

2 teaspoons dried marjoram

2 teaspoons ground dried rosemary

¼ teaspoon nutmeg

1 tablespoon dried oregano

2 teaspoons fresh lemon juice

Salt and pepper to taste

2½ pounds venison, cut into
  ¼-inch strips

1 (12-ounce) package pita breads

1 cup Tzatziki Sauce (recipe below)

6 ounces Feta cheese, crumbled

½ head of lettuce, chopped

2 tomatoes, sliced

In a large bowl, whisk together the olive oil, cumin, garlic, shallots, marjoram, rosemary, nutmeg, oregano, lemon juice, salt and pepper. Add the venison strips and coat evenly. Cover bowl with plastic wrap and marinate in the refrigerator no less than 2 hours, 4 hours is best.

Heat a large skillet to medium-high heat. Drain excess marinade from venison strips and cook, half pound at a time, until the meat has browned, about 6 to 8 minutes. The inside should be medium-well to well done.

Warm pita bread. Place venison on pita, drizzle with 2 tablespoons Tzatziki sauce. Top with 1½ tablespoons Feta cheese, lettuce and tomato.

YIELD: 6 SANDWICHES

TZATZIKI SAUCE

1 cup plain Greek yogurt, sour
  cream or créme fraiche

½ lemon, juiced

¼ cup finely chopped
  cucumber without seeds

Salt to taste

Combine ingredients and whisk to mix thoroughly.

Farmers' Market Hero

Malley Sisson, administrative dietitian in dining services, is a familiar face at the farmers' market each summer in Manhattan. Head to her booth first. She sells out of her scones, tomato cheese tarts with homegrown garlic and inventive jams. Ms. Sisson is known for creative cookery and her use of produce from her garden. This recipe says summer. But be warned: although it makes 12 servings, it feeds only 6 or so. People demand second and third helpings. You can make it with frozen corn but go for the fresh if possible. She seasons the crumb mixture with Penzy's Northwoods Seasoning, a blend of herbs and spices such as chipotle pepper and rosemary.

Ms. Sisson was food service director at the K-State Union from February 1980 to May 1996 when food service was contracted out.

FARMERS' MARKET SUMMER CASSEROLE ✧ ✧

By Malley Sisson

4 ears sweet corn, raw, cut off cob

2 cups heavy cream

3 medium green zucchini, cut in ¼-inch slices (about 18 ounces)

3 medium yellow squash, cut in ¼-inch slices (about 18 ounces)

3 tablespoons unsalted butter, melted, divided

1 teaspoon salt

1 teaspoon black pepper

6 ounces cheese food such as Cheez Whiz or Velveeta

2 large green onions, thinly sliced

¾ teaspoon dried dill weed

24 butter crackers such as Ritz (1 sleeve), crushed

Preheat oven to 350°F.

Cut corn from cob scraping both kernels and milk into medium saucepan. Add cream and cook over medium heat until mixture is reduced by about a third.

Toss zucchini and yellow squash with 2 tablespoons butter, salt and pepper and spread on cookie sheet. Bake for 15–20 minutes, stirring occasionally.

To creamed corn mixture, add cheese, onions and dill weed. Stir to blend and pour in large mixing bowl. Add squash mixture and stir lightly. Taste and adjust seasoning.

Pour into 2-quart casserole dish.

In small saucepan melt remaining tablespoon butter. Stir in cracker crumbs and sprinkle over casserole. Bake for 40 to 45 minutes or until edges begin to bubble.

YIELD: 12 SERVINGS

The Cookery Collection Cook

Roger Adams, special collections librarian at Hale Library, is caretaker of the Cookery Collection. Ranked among the foremost collections in the nation, it contains more than 15,000 cookbooks and related volumes, works dating from 1487 to *Teatime to Tailgates*.

Adams cooks, bakes and brews. His Grand Aunt Ruth Ellen Warfield Reynolds, born in 1906 in Lincoln County, Kentucky, taught him to make cheese grits. He adapted the tomato jam and paired it with the grits. "I don't know why we eat so much seafood in Kentucky—not having an ocean—but we do," he said.

✤✤ CHEESE GRITS WITH SHRIMP, BACON AND TOMATO JAM HIGHLIGHTS

By Roger Adams

1 cup stone ground grits (white or yellow; I prefer yellow)
4 cups water
Salt and white pepper
4 tablespoons unsalted butter
1½ cups shredded sharp cheddar cheese

6–8 slices bacon (I typically use thick-sliced strongly smoked bacon or peppered bacon, hence the 6 slices)
1 pound shrimp, peeled and deveined
2 cloves garlic, minced
6–8 scallions, sliced on the bias ⅓-inch thick

First, prepare the grits. In a heavy sauce pan, bring the water to a boil and slowly whisk in the grits. Season with salt and white pepper to taste. Reduce the heat and allow to simmer stirring continuously until cooked, usually about 15–20 minutes. Do not cheat and use instant grits! Remove from the heat and stir in the butter and cheese, both will melt nicely. Cover with a plate to keep warm.

Slice the bacon in ½-inch pieces. In a frying pan, cook bacon until crisp. Reserve the bacon on a paper bag to drain.

Add shrimp and garlic to the remaining bacon drippings and cook quickly, just until the shrimp are pink; do not overcook the shrimp or the garlic. Add the scallions near the end of the cooking time for the shrimp, usually just about 1 minute to wilt them. Draining the bacon drippings from the shrimp, garlic and scallions would be a crime, so don't do it. Fold this mixture into the cheese grits, transfer to a large bowl and top with the reserved bacon.

Serve immediately allowing each person to have some tomato jam on the side.

YIELD: 6 SERVINGS (LEFTOVERS UNLIKELY)

TOMATO JAM

1 cup fire roasted canned, chopped or diced tomatoes	1 tablespoon corn syrup
½ cup rice wine vinegar	2 teaspoons minced garlic (usually 2 cloves)
2 tablespoons brown sugar	½ teaspoon ground coriander

Combine all the ingredients in a small sauce pan and bring to a boil. Reduce heat and allow to simmer, stirring occasionally allowing most of the tomato juice to evaporate; this is usually 20–25 minutes. Remove from heat and allow to cool to room temperature or slightly warm when serving.

·11·

Tailgates
in
Willie's Backyard

Recipes

CHARLES GOODNIGHT INVENTED tailgating. Only then food was called chuck and it came from the chuck wagon. In 1866 Goodnight, a Texas Panhandle rancher and general man-about-the-country, bought a U.S. Army Studebaker wagon and outfitted it as a rolling kitchen cupboard from which the camp cookie could feed hungry cowboys on the trail from Texas to the railhead in Dodge City, Kansas.

Tailgating is ritual at K-State. An estimated 35,000 to 40,000 people dine in parking lots and the fields surrounding Bill Synder Family Stadium before football games. Some don't even go to the games, instead watching on television from their parking lot dining room.

After World War II, station wagons were the tailgating vehicles of choice. Roam the area around the stadium today and spy $100,000 RVs, discount-store awnings, huddles of cars and more pickups than outside a rodeo arena. See satellite dishes, refrigerators, grills and a sea of blinding purple.

First You Put on Purple, Then You Make a Roux

David Fallin, professor in marketing, hails from Louisiana. Tailgate cooking to him means gumbo and his gumbo, attests spouse Jana Fallin, is legendary. It won a gumbo cook-off in Lafayette, Louisiana. Fallin has been known to rig up enough Coleman stoves and burners to accommodate a giant pot for gumbo and another for rice. One year several of the K-State football players were from Louisiana, some of them in Fallin's class. After the game, they came out to the parking lot to get "a taste of home." "Those are sweet memories," Jana Fallin said. She is director of the Center for the Advancement of Teaching and Learning and a university distinguished teaching scholar in music education.

❖❖ DAVID FALLIN'S LEGENDARY
CHICKEN AND SAUSAGE GUMBO

2 pounds boneless chicken breast

2 stalks celery

3 bay leaves

Chicken stock

½ cup cooking oil

½ cup flour

4 quarts water

2 pounds andouille or polish
    kielbasa, sliced

1 large purple onion, chopped

1 bell pepper, red or green, diced

2 pods garlic, peeled and minced

2 stalks celery with leaves,
    chopped

¼ cup green onions, chopped

¼ cup parsley, minced

Cajun seasoning

Tabasco

Cooked rice

In a crockpot, cook chicken, celery, bay leaves and enough water or chicken broth to cover on low for 8 to 10 hours. Cool and remove chicken. Throw out liquid.

Shred or cube the chicken.

TO MAKE ROUX:

Heat oil in a cast iron skillet over low heat. When warm and fluid, add flour and stir constantly until brown (this may take at least 30 minutes); immediately remove from heat. Set aside until cool, stirring often to prevent separation. If it burns even slightly (black flecks will appear), throw it out and start over again.

In large cooking pot dissolve roux in water over medium-high heat and let boil for 20–30 minutes. Stir frequently to avoid sticking and to make sure roux is completely dissolved.

Add chicken, sausage, onion, bell pepper, garlic and celery. Bring to a boil. Lower heat to medium-low and cook about 1 hour.

Once vegetables are tender, add green onions and parsley and cook an additional 15 minutes. Season with your favorite Cajun seasoning and Tabasco.

Serve over steamed white rice in gumbo (soup) bowls.

You may add gumbo file (ground sassafras) to thicken gumbo.

YIELD: 6 TO 8 SERVINGS

A Friend Is Someone Who Shares Recipes

Jet Tila had never been to Kansas before he signed on to do the Culinary Enhancement Workshop in 2007. The workshop, created by Missy Schrader, instructor for the Department of Hospitality Management and Dietetics and a dietitian for housing and dining services, was 7 years old and had a glowing reputation.

At the annual two sessions of the workshop, guest chefs talked about their featured cuisines and demonstrated cooking techniques, followed by lunch based on the chefs' recipes and a hands-on session. The first session drew amateur cooks and working professionals who could apply for continuing education credits for Kansas dietitian licensure. The second was strictly for students.

In 2007, Chef Tila taught a how to roll sushi workshop. He also led the workshop in 2009.

Chef Tila, a nationally celebrated chef conversant in all styles of Asian cuisine, learned his craft from his Cantonese grandmother at the family restaurant, Le Cordon Blue and the California Sushi Academy. He has appeared on many television and radio food shows; his recipes have been published in *Bon Appetit* and other magazines.

In 2011 he received Human Ecology's Friend of the College Award. He wasn't at the Celebration of Excellence to pick up his honor: he was filming *Iron Chef* in New York.

In 2012 he opened Charleston, which features American comfort food from an Asian cuisine perspective, in Santa Monica, California. He holds the Guinness World Record for the World's Largest Stir-Fry—4,010 pounds. We didn't ask for that recipe although it's an imaginative idea for a tailgate party.

KOREAN GALBI SHORT RIBS

By Jet Tila

½ cup soy sauce	4 pounds short ribs, sliced
⅓ cup brown sugar	3–4 green onions, chopped
2 tablespoons sesame oil	2–3 tablespoons toasted
3–4 garlic cloves, minced	sesame seeds
Salt and pepper to taste	

Combine soy sauce, brown sugar, sesame oil and garlic in a large bowl. Marinate short ribs in soy sauce mixture about 30 to 60 minutes.

Heat an outdoor grill or indoor grill pan until very hot.

Drain ribs and season with salt and pepper as desired. Grill over high heat until meat reaches desired doneness, about 5 to 8 minutes for medium-rare. Sprinkle with sesame seeds and scallions.

Yield: 4 to 6 servings

BEER CAN CHICKEN WITH CHIPOTLE CREMA ✤✤

By Jet Tila

2 whole chickens
Olive oil
2 cans beer
Flour tortillas

RUB:

2 tablespoons ground cumin
2 tablespoons ground chili powder
2 teaspoons garlic powder
2 teaspoons salt
1 teaspoon ground black pepper

CREMA:

2 cups Mexican crema (or
    sour cream)
Juice and zest of one lime
½ cup chopped cilantro
2 tablespoons chopped canned
    chipotle pepper, plus more
    as needed
Salt and pepper

To make rub, combine cumin, chili powder, garlic powder, salt and pepper in a small bowl. Heat an outdoor grill or indoor grill pan until medium hot.

Remove neck and giblets and discard. Rub chicken inside and out with oil then the rub.

Open beer can and take several gulps (make them big gulps so that the can is half full). Place beer can on a solid surface. Grabbing a chicken leg in each hand, plunk the bird cavity over the beer can. Transfer the bird-on-a-can to the center of the grill, balancing the bird on its 2 legs and the can like a tripod. Repeat with the second chicken.

Cook the chicken over medium-high, indirect heat (i.e. no coals or burners directly under the bird), with the grill cover on, for 1¼ hours or until the internal temperature registers 165°F in the breast area and 180°F in the thigh, or until the thigh juice runs clear when stabbed with a sharp knife. Let rest for 10 minutes before carving.

Meanwhile, combine crema, lime zest and juice, cilantro and chipotle in a small bowl. Mix with salt and pepper.

Carve chicken into pieces and serve with grilled tortillas or cut chicken off the bones and wrap meat in warm tortillas. Serve with crema.

YIELD: 4 TO 6 SERVINGS

Never Enough Purple

Ask Carl and Mary Ice what they like about K-State and then take a comfortable seat—it will take a while. They are fans of the students, professors, the leadership, the campus, Justin Hall, the student opportunities and, of course, the Wildcat teams.

"When we tailgate, we heat the chili to boiling and carefully transfer the pot to a lined cardboard box for transporting to the stadium. It will cool to a comfortable temperature in approximately 60–90 minutes," explains the 1980 graduate in home economics education with a master's degree in adult occupational continuing education. Carl Ice has a 1979 degree in industrial engineering. Both are active alumni leaders and generous in their support.

She serves her chili with any combination of the following: corn bread muffins, corn chips, tortilla chips, sour cream, chopped green onions, grated cheese, jalapenos and avocados. This chili is best made the day before the game.

✤✤ MARY ICE'S TURKEY CHILI

2 pounds ground turkey breast
1 medium onion, chopped
1 medium green pepper, chopped
1 tablespoon minced garlic
1 tablespoon chili powder
1½ teaspoons coarsely ground
    black pepper

2 (15-ounce) cans black beans,
    drained and rinsed
2 (15-ounce) cans petite diced
    tomatoes
1 (6-ounce) can tomato paste
64 ounces tomato juice

Spray a large skillet with cooking spray and brown together the turkey, onion, green pepper and garlic.

Add chili powder and ground pepper. Add black beans, diced tomatoes and tomato paste. Stir well. Transfer to a large pot or crock pot and stir in the tomato juice, mixing thoroughly. Heat to the desired temperature before serving.

Yield: 6 servings

STOP ME IF YOU'VE HEARD THE ONE ABOUT
THE PLEDGE CLASS AND THE HOG ROAST

Many might know this story because similar ones have been told around campus over the decades. Hog roasts are popular at K-State—the meat lab provides hogs for tailgates, residence halls celebrations and other events such as fraternity traditions.

As was the custom, the freshmen at Beta Theta Pi were in charge of the annual hog roast. Drew Hanson and the rest of the pledge class of 1976 headed to Tuttle Creek park on a Monday evening to "dig a pit, toss in a slaughtered hog, light a fire and watch it until the Friday evening when all the fraternity members, their dates and the housemother would arrive for a feast."

He continues: "Being freshmen, we were 'know-it-all's' and didn't need to be told how to roast a hog (not that I recall a. anyone offering to teach us or b. we might have actually admitted our woeful ignorance by asking, 'So how does one roast a hog?')"

The Beta Theta Pi brothers found a secluded spot out of the sight of park rangers, gathered wood and started digging. They secured two large pieces of tin: one went under the hog, the other on top. They tended the fire faithfully throughout the week. "Great male-bonding time," Hanson notes. On Friday they decided to douse the fire and start preparing the feast. Hanson continues,

After extinguishing the coals and removing them from the pit, we carefully yet expectantly lifted the top layer of tin off our evening meal. Time seemed to stand still as each freshman looked at each other then at unrecognizable black charred fragments of what once had been a promising meal. We had forgotten to shovel a thick layer of dirt back onto the top layer of tin, thereby providing a good bed of insulation from the soaring heat of the burning logs and allowing a low slow simmering heat to gradually roast the meat instead of 'torching' the meat. Our dazed expressions of disbelief at what we were seeing quickly morphed into expressions of terror! Everyone (the housemother too!) was going to be here in 4 hours expecting succulent hog and lots of it!

Why not turn the disaster into a hot dog roast? Several young men dashed into Manhattan for supplies. "The upperclassmen seemed to take it all in stride…almost as if this sort of catastrophe had happened before…some had even brought Vista burgers and fries for themselves and their dates," Hanson notes. The housemother said the hot dogs were the best she'd ever tasted.

The story rested silently for 35 years.

Then recently, he and his wife Brenda met Terry and Sandy, new members of their church. "How did you two meet?" the Hansons innocently asked. Terry and Sandy looked at each other and started laughing.

They were on a blind date in Manhattan and someone sold them two tickets to a hog roast for $10. The fraternity event was at Tuttle Creek 35 years ago and the entrée was a "far-too-well-done-hog." "These dufus freshmen tried to salvage the night with hot dogs and hot dog buns," Terry explained, adding that if he ever saw the guy that sold him those two tickets, he was getting his money back one way or the other!

Hanson nudged his wife to quietly exit but not before she could whisper to Sandy, "I don't know who sold Terry the tickets, but I think I know the chef!"

From the Gardens to Tailgates

Vickie James, a K-State trained dietitian who directs the much-lauded Healthy Kids Challenge, writes about friendship, gardens and a Mexican cuisine themed tailgate party with her friend Claudia Hohnbaum:

Growing up on a western Kansas farm, a huge vegetable garden was simply part of summer's activities. From preparing the garden to harvesting and canning the delicious results, it was a treasured time.

My husband and I continued the tradition with our two kids when they were growing up. My mom loved it because by that time, health limitations kept her from doing all the

Emma Thurston, a graduate of Hoeflin Stone House Early Childhood Education Center, prefers watermelon. PHOTOGRAPH BY JANE P. MARSHALL

tasks that nurturing a garden required but she could still can and freeze circles around me! She eagerly waited for me to bring her buckets of juicy ripe tomatoes, which she canned for awesome winter time chili and stews. Mountains of yellow and purple onions and green peppers were frozen for use in favorite family casseroles.

One fall I asked my friend Claudia, who was visiting from Wichita, to drop some tomatoes, onions and peppers at my mom's house in Dighton since she was going that way. Hours later, long after Claudia should have been the produce delivery wagon, my mom called to see where the veggies were. She was ready to can! Claudia had stopped by Mom's but she forgot to leave the produce!

All was not lost. Claudia froze the 'stolen produce' and later turned it into a tailgate treasure. We call our group the KSU Maniacs. We feed 40 to 65 family and friends at each game. Mom's tomatoes and onions, we figured, called for a Mexican cuisine theme. Aaahh, yes, chicken enchiladas!

Now we have to reproduce the meal every fall and Claudia has to bring her infamous chicken enchiladas! While still yummy, we all agree they will never be as wonderful as the year she prepared them with our family's 'stolen' garden produce! (Oh, and we did make sure my mom got a pan of the enchiladas, too!)

CLAUDIA HOHNBAUM'S KSU ❖❖ TAILGATE CHICKEN ENCHILADAS

From Vickie James

SALSA:

15–20 James family fresh, ripe garden tomatoes

1 fresh jalapeno pepper, finely chopped

1 fresh green pepper, finely chopped

4–6 green onions chopped or 1 large yellow onion chopped

1 teaspoon garlic salt

1 tablespoon finely chopped cilantro

FILLING:

1 pound cooked, diced chicken

1 cup salsa

½ cup light cream cheese

8 flour tortillas

TOPPING:

⅔ cup salsa

1 (8-ounce) can tomato sauce

2 tablespoons taco seasoning mix

8 ounces grated Monterey Jack or Cheddar cheese

SALSA:

Skin tomatoes and chop. Add peppers, onions, garlic salt and cilantro. Cook on stovetop until sauce is thick. It will cook down to about ⅔ of original volume.

FILLING:

Mix diced chicken and salsa. Spread about 1 tablespoon cream cheese on each tortilla. Top with an eighth of the chicken mixture. Roll up each tortilla; don't tuck the ends, keep them open.

Place in a 9 x 13-inch baking dish.

TOPPING:

Mix salsa, tomato sauce and seasoning mix. Pour over tortillas just before you are ready to bake. Top with grated cheese.

Cover loosely with foil and bake at 325°F for 25–30 minutes.

YIELD: 8 ENCHILADAS

✣✣ CAROLINA STYLE PULLED PORK SANDWICH

From K-State Dining Services

1 (4–5 pound) Boston
    butt roast

RUB:
4 teaspoons salt
2 tablespoons brown sugar
⅛ teaspoon chipotle powder
1 tablespoon rubbed sage
2½ teaspoons garlic powder

SAUCE:
1 teaspoon salt
½ cup plus 1 tablespoon
    brown sugar
⅛ teaspoon chipotle powder
1 teaspoon sage
1 teaspoon garlic powder
2¼ cups cider vinegar
4 ounces canned jalapeno
    slices, drained

Blend ingredients for rub and press over entire surface of the roast. Cover with plastic film and refrigerate for 24 hours at or below 40°F.

Preheat oven to 250°F. Remove plastic and place roast in baking pan. Tent pan loosely with foil, leaving ends open. Roast for 5 to 6 hours. Remove from oven and cover tightly with foil. Let sit for at least 30 minutes.

Place sauce ingredients in saucepan while pork is roasting. Bring to a boil over medium heat. Reduce heat and simmer for 10 minutes. Strain out jalapenos and set aside.

Cut roasts in 1½ to 2 inch thick slices. Shred slices with two forks or gloved fingers, removing bone and fat. Place shredded pork in pan and pour reserved vinegar sauce over the pork. Toss well to allow sauce to coat the pork.

Serve on buns with coleslaw, sliced onions and pickles.

YIELD: 40 SERVINGS

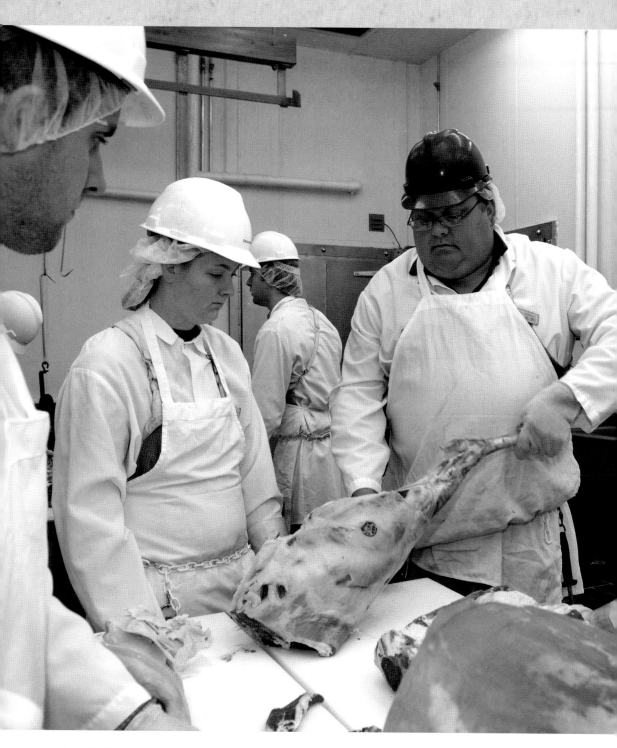

John Wolf teaches students about meat cuts in the meat lab in Weber Hall. He also roasts whole hogs for tailgate events. COURTESY OF DAVID MAYES, KANSAS STATE UNIVERSITY DIVISION OF COMMUNICATIONS AND MARKETING

A Detour Off the Santa Fe Trail to Bill Synder Family Stadium

The Hays House in Council Grove claims to be the oldest continuously operating restaurant west of the Mississippi River. The founder was Seth Hays, the great-grandson of Daniel Boone, cousin of Kit Carson and trader who supplied travelers on the Santa Fe Trail beginning in 1847. He built the current building in 1857.

Helen Judd is granddaughter to the Whitings who bought the building in 1911. In 1974 she and her husband Charlie restored it and took over the restaurant. Their daughter, Kathy Judd Kurtz, graduated from K-State and took a job at Kikkoman where she developed Western Lite Broil.

The Hays House is still in business (although with new owners) and still famous for fried chicken, burgers, steaks and desserts.

✥✥ WESTERN LITE BROIL
By Kathy Judd Kurtz

1½ **pounds lean beef such as flank, top round or sirloin steak**
½ **cup soy sauce**
¼ **cup water**

2 **tablespoons lemon juice**
2 **tablespoons honey**
1 **teaspoon dry onion flakes**
¼ **teaspoon garlic powder**

Combine soy sauce, water, juice, honey, onion flakes and garlic powder. Pour it over meat, cover tightly and marinate in the refrigerator for 24 to 48 hours.

Broil or grill to desired doneness. Serve thinly sliced.

Yield: 6 servings

Wild About Wildcats and Chocolate

If Sally Yahnke, family and consumer sciences education associate professor, isn't hollering at Snyder Family Stadium during football season, she can be found in front of her television set surrounded by fellow fans hollering. She's known for her culinary adventures and these brownies, so rich and unusual, are always on her football buffets.

SALLY'S TOUCHDOWN BROWNIES ❖❖

From Sally Yahnke

1½ cups (3 sticks) unsalted butter	2 cups sugar
2 cups cocoa, natural or Dutch process	2 cups packed brown sugar
	2 tablespoons vanilla
6 eggs	2 cups flour
	1 teaspoon kosher salt

Preheat oven to 350°F. Line a 9 x 13 pan with parchment or foil and spray with nonstick cooking spray.

Melt butter in medium saucepan over medium heat. Remove from heat and stir in cocoa. Let cool slightly. In large bowl, whisk the eggs then add sugars and vanilla. Stir. Add slightly cooled chocolate mixture then fold in the flour and salt until just combined. Don't over mix.

Spread the batter evenly in the pan. Bake 40 to 45 minutes or until a crust forms and a toothpick inserted into the center comes out mostly clean.

Cool on a wire rack before cutting into pieces.

YIELD: 24 BROWNIES

·12·

Celebrate!

Recipes

K-State, like most of Kansas, needs only a twilight of an excuse to cover a table with food. A football game. A graduation. A retirement. A welcome to K-State. A success. A weekend. A sunny day.

Or a birthday.

This chapter offers recipes for celebrations big and small. Some were created especially for *Teatime to Tailgates*. Some are traditional for celebrations. Some you probably won't try at home. But with each, we salute K-State and its 150 years of feeding the campus and influencing the cuisine of the world.

With President Kirk Schulz presiding, Kansas State University kicked off its sesquicentennial celebration on February 14, 2013, in typical K-State style: food, music, displays, speeches, and renditions of *Wabash Cannonball* and the *Fight Song* that nearly blew the windows out of Ahearn Field House.

The student a cappella vocal ensemble In-A-Chord serenaded sweetly with the *Alma Mater* before busting out with "Fighting ever fighting for a Wildcat victory!" Most impressive was their voices-only rendition of *Wabash Cannonball*.

Although Willie the Wildcat is not 150 years old, he was there high-fiving students, teasing children and getting his photo taken more often than the yell leaders. The K-State football team was nicknamed Wildcats in 1915 by Coach John Bender. The name changed to "Farmers" in 1916 but Head Coach Charles Bachman reinstated Wildcats in 1920.

The 9-month celebration, which included a purple-infused gala at the Hilton Garden Inn convention center, has been on the drawing board for more than 2 years. More than 100 committee members divided into 13 sub-committees and hundreds more faculty, staff and students contributed.

The kick-off event consumed more than 400 volunteers, 5,000 cupcakes and 300 gallons of Birthday Ice Cream.

Willie the Wildcat isn't the only one wild about K-State ice cream. Courtesy of David Mayes, Kansas State University Division of Communications and Marketing

Cake and Ice Cream...Lots of It

A birthday party must have ice cream and cake and K-State is famous nationwide for its ice cream.

K-State ice cream, in purple Willie-adorned cartons, is only available in Manhattan and the prime outlet is Call Hall, which opened in 1964, where it is manufactured in the K-State plant. Each year the plant produces about 15,000 gallons of ice cream in more than 35 different flavors, most of them invented by students. Vanilla is the most popular, says Renee Westgate, KSU Dairy Bar manager.

To make "Wildcat Birthday 150" ice cream, frozen at the rate of 100 gallons an hour, the dairy plant mixes white ice cream with cake batter-based flavoring, pieces of birthday cake and purple sprinkles.

"We use a No. 10 can of cake batter base for every 15 gallons of ice cream mix," said Jared Parsons, plant manager. He adds frozen colored cake pieces and royal purple sprinkles, which he buys in bulk.

The dairy bar, originally opened in 1905 in the basement of Anderson Hall, also sells milk, cheese, butter, selected meat from the KSU Meat Lab, eggs and milling products such as flour and wheat germ. It moved to Waters Hall in 1923, then to Call Hall in 1964.

Birthday cake for the sesquicentennial kick-off came in the form of cupcakes, some of them made by Derby Dining Services. This is that recipe. For the event, dining service bakers topped each cupcake with a white chocolate Powercat.

At the Dairy Processing Plant, students learn to make products such as ice cream, cheese and butter. Courtesy of David Mayes, Kansas State University Division of Communications and Marketing

WILDCAT CHOCOLATE CUPCAKES ✤✤

From K-State Dining Services

27.53 pounds cake flour

5.197 pounds cocoa

42.208 pounds sugar

2.753 pounds non-fat dry milk solids

.913 pounds salt

1.099 pounds baking powder

.557 pounds baking soda

36.716 pounds water (divided)

17.137 pounds cake shortening

.371 pounds vanilla extract

20.1823 pounds whole liquid eggs

Preheat oven to 350°F and put 1,500 cupcake liners in muffin tins.

Combine and thoroughly mix flour, cocoa, sugar, milk solids, salt, baking powder and baking soda. Add 14.074 pounds water and the shortening. Mix at low speed for one minute then at medium speed for 3 minutes. Scrape bowl and paddle. Add 12.852 pounds water and vanilla.

Mix on low for a minute and at medium speed for two minutes. Blend in eggs and 9.79 pounds of water. Mix at low speed for two minutes.

Divide into cupcake liners and bake for 15 minutes until cupcakes test done. Cool and ice with Chocolate Creamed Frosting (recipe below) and top with purple and white sprinkles.

YIELD: 1,500 CUPCAKES

CHOCOLATE CREAMED FROSTING

9.458 pounds evaporated milk

4.542 pounds margarine

29.801 pounds confectioners' sugar (divided)

2.981 pounds cocoa

.047 pounds salt

.047 pounds vanilla extract

Place milk, margarine, 11.826 pounds sugar, cocoa and salt in mixer bowl and blend thoroughly. Add vanilla and remaining 17.975 pounds sugar and mix slowly until blended, then at medium speed until light.

Possibly the World's Best Cheesecake

Deb Canter, professor and registered dietitian, has been known to bribe people with her cheesecakes. She ships them all over the country when she donates them to fundraisers and fills special requests. One thing the much-awarded professor is not known to do is share her coveted recipe. But she has a generous heart and a passion for food history, so she said "yes" when we begged.

❖❖ DEB'S CLASSIC CHEESECAKE

Created by Deb Canter

CRUST:

1¾ cups graham cracker
  crumbs

¼ cup granulated sugar

5½ tablespoons melted butter

FILLING:

4 large whole eggs

1 cup granulated sugar

1 teaspoon vanilla

3 (8-ounce) packages cream
  cheese, softened

TOPPING:

2 cups sour cream

¾ cup sugar

Preheat oven to 350°F. Line the bottom of a 9-inch springform pan with parchment paper.

CRUST:

Mix together ingredients and press mixture into the bottom and ½ way up the sides of the springform pan. Set aside.

FILLING:

Mix ingredients until smooth in a stand-mixer using the flat paddle attachment or using a hand-mixer. Avoid mixing too much air into the batter.

Pour the mixture into the graham cracker crust and bake at 350°F for 50–55 minutes until lightly browned. Don't worry if it cracks slightly. Set aside to cool for about 30 minutes. Meanwhile, turn the oven temperature up to 425°F.

TOPPING:

Mix ingredients together and pour over the cooled filling, spreading the topping to the edges of the pan. Bake in the 425°F oven for 10 minutes.

Remove the cheesecake from the oven and place it immediately into the refrigerator. Chill at least 12 hours before portioning.

Loosen the cheesecake from the pan by running a thin knife around the edge of the cheesecake. Unlock the pan and remove the sides of the pan. Using a long knife, carefully slide the knife blade between the graham cracker crust and the parchment paper. Gently move the knife around to loosen the crust from the parchment paper. Slide the cheesecake onto a cardboard cake round or serving platter.

Run the blade of the long knife under hot water and then slice the cheesecake in half. Cleaning the knife under hot water after each cut, cut the cake into fourths, then into eighths, then into 16 pieces.

Serve as is or top with your favorite fresh fruit, canned fruit pie filling or other toppings.

YIELD: 16 SERVINGS

Baking with Grandma: The Gift that Keeps on Giving

Stetson Honig, Hugoton, was 10 years old when he won the Youth Division Artistic Award in the 2004 Kansas Wheat Commission competition. He had a little help from his grandmother, Frances Russell, who taught him to bake bread when Stetson was 7. "I grew up in 4-H so I have been baking constantly since then, although I don't get to much anymore," he said. Stetson is a student at K-State because "I basically grew up brainwashed by three generations of K-Staters." Mrs. Russell, a K-State graduate in home economics, was housemother for Farm House and for Sigma Chi for many years.

Loaves of bread were made from the new hard red winter wheat variety named "1863" to commemorate the year K-State opened as the nation's first operational land-grant university under the Morrill Act, 2013. COURTESY OF DAVID MAYES, KANSAS STATE UNIVERSITY DIVISION OF COMMUNICATIONS AND MARKETING

WILDCAT SWIRL BREAD ✤ ✤

From Stetson Honig

1½ cups water (80°F)	4 cups bread flour
2 tablespoons vegetable oil	1½ teaspoons active dry
2 tablespoons sugar	yeast
2 teaspoons salt	2 teaspoons violet paste
2 tablespoons dry milk	food coloring

To make swirl bread, prepare the above recipe twice using a bread maker on the dough cycle. One recipe is white, the second is purple.

Put water, oil, sugar, salt, dry milk, flour and yeast in the bread machine pan. Start bread on dough cycle. Check dough after 5 minutes. If it is too dry, add ½–1 tablespoon water; if too wet, add 1 tablespoon of flour at a time. When cycle is completed, place dough in a sealable plastic bag sprayed with nonstick cooking spray. Refrigerate dough.

To prepare purple dough, add violet food coloring to the 1½ cups water. Stir until dissolved. Continue recipe as above.

Remove white dough from refrigerator 30 minutes before purple dough is completed. Preheat oven to 350°F.

Divide both white and purple dough in half. Roll white dough into two 16 x 8-inch rectangles. Roll purple dough into two 14 x 6-inch rectangles. Place one purple rectangle on top of one white rectangle. Roll up tightly; seal with fingertips as you roll. Pinch seam and ends under loaf. Repeat to make second loaf.

Place loaves, seam-side down, in two greased 9 x 5-inch loaf pans. Cover; let rise until double in warm 90°F place. Optional: for a shiny crust, beat 1 whole egg and 1 tablespoon water together and brush on loaves.

Bake for 35 to 40 minutes or until done. Tent top of loaves with foil last 5 minutes to prevent over-browning. Remove from pans; cool on rack.

YIELD: 2 LOAVES

Sauerkraut Balls: The Life of the Party

"You have to include Marian Spears' Sauerkraut Balls," Betsy Barrett demanded. "They don't sound good but they are the best thing I ever put in my mouth." Dr. Barrett, who taught the first wine courses at K-State, has taste buds one can trust. She and husband Pat Pesci, who directed the hospitality management program for many years, entertain in their home on Hudson Street with lavish spreads of food and creative wine selections.

Dr. Spears, professor and head of the Department of Dietetics, Restaurant and Institutional Management, retired in 1975 after 24 years on the faculty. Sauerkraut Balls were on the menu of her famous annual Christmas party. "She had an open bar with a professional bartender and hired dietetic students to fry the hors d'oeuvres all evening so they could keep a stream of hot ones all the time," remembered Deb Canter. "That party always had wonderful food, and it was the place to be," PhD alumnus Mary Gregoire echoed the sentiment.

SAUERKRAUT BALLS ✤✤

By Marian C. Spears

¼ pound ground pork sausage

¼ pound ground cooked ham

¼ pound ground cooked corned beef

¼ cup finely chopped onion

½ teaspoon finely chopped parsley

1 cup all-purpose flour

½ teaspoon salt

½ teaspoon dry mustard

1 cup milk

3 cups firmly packed sauerkraut, well drained and chopped fine

3 cups fresh bread crumbs

Melted shortening or oil for deep frying

EGG BATTER:

2 eggs, beaten

⅔ cup water

1 teaspoon salt

Break up pork sausage into small bits and fry in a heavy skillet until lightly browned. Add ground ham and corned beef, chopped onion and parsley; continue to cook, stirring frequently until thoroughly heated.

Sift flour, salt and mustard together and add to meat mixture, stirring constantly to combine. Add milk and continue to cook over low heat until mixture is thickened. Remove from heat. Stir in chopped sauerkraut and mix well.

Chill mixture thoroughly. (For rapid chilling, spread in a shallow pan and place in freezer for 30 minutes.) Shape mixture into ¾-inch balls. Roll lightly in flour.

Combine beaten eggs, water and salt and blend to make egg batter. Dip floured balls into egg batter, then in fresh breadcrumbs. Deep fry in 360°F oil for 1½ to 2 minutes or until golden brown.

Drain on absorbent paper and serve hot with mustard sauce.

YIELD: 75 SAUERKRAUT BALLS

Let Us Eat Cake...Rachel Benjamin's

Rachel Benjamin believes that "cake fixes everything." Owner and baker at 4 Cakes, she calls her custom dessert business a descendant of Manhattan's 4 Olives Restaurant and Wine Bar.

4 Olives, owned by Rachel and Chef Scott Benjamin, is one of Manhattan's celebration destinations. At the restaurant, where she is pastry chef, and in her baking business, she makes everything from scratch and never freezes her cakes. This is her most requested birthday cake, by customers as well as her own children.

❖❖ RED VELVET CAKE WITH CINNAMON CREAM CHEESE FROSTING
From Rachel Benjamin for 4 Cakes

1½ cups vegetable oil	1⅓ cups sugar
1 cup buttermilk	3 tablespoons Dutch processed
2 large eggs	cocoa powder
2 tablespoons red food coloring	¾ teaspoon salt
2 teaspoons apple cider vinegar	1 teaspoon baking soda
2½ cups all-purpose flour	

Preheat oven to 350°F. Prepare 2 8-inch cake pans with at least 2-inch sides. Spray pans with baking spray, line bottom with parchment and flour sides.

Mix oil, buttermilk, eggs, food coloring and vinegar in bowl with stand mixer. Sift flour, sugar, cocoa, salt and baking soda. Pour dry ingredients over wet mixture. Mix on medium speed for 2 to 3 minutes. Divide cake batter between pans.

Bake 35–40 minutes or until pick comes out clean. When cool, ice with Cinnamon Cream Cheese Frosting.

CINNAMON CREAM CHEESE FROSTING

8 ounces cream cheese, room temperature

½ cup unsalted butter, room temperature

¼ cup vegetable shortening

½ tablespoon vanilla

¼ teaspoon salt

1½–1¾ pounds powdered sugar

2 teaspoons ground cinnamon

Blend cream cheese, butter and shortening in stand mixer until smooth. Add vanilla and salt, mix until smooth. Blend in powdered sugar until smooth. Add cinnamon and blend until smooth.

This frosting will "crust" over a bit, allowing for a completely smooth finish. If you prefer a finish that is swirly and not set, omit the shortening. Garnish with Red Hot candies.

YIELD: 1 CAKE

Punch Without the Punch

This mock champagne punch originated with Grace Shugart and has been published in many editions of *Food for Fifty*. If you prefer something a bit less sweet, the 7th edition has a recipe for Sauerkraut Juice Cocktail.

❖❖ PINK CHAMPAGNE-STYLE PUNCH

From Food for Fifty *(2001)*

2 quarts water	½ cup fresh lemon juice
2⅞ cups sugar	1¼ cups grenadine syrup
2 quarts unsweetened red grapefruit juice	7 quarts ginger ale

Heat water and sugar until sugar dissolves. Cool. Add grapefruit juice, lemon juice and grenadine syrup. Refrigerate until ready to serve.

Just before serving combine the chilled juice mixture with chilled ginger ale. Ladle punch into champagne classes and garnish with a strip of lemon peel.

YIELD: 96 (½ CUP) SERVINGS OR 3 GALLONS

Celebration Punch

In spring 1964, Mary Jeanne Scoby Jensen was in charge of the beverage for the event honoring matriculating home economics graduate students. "It turned out good so I sent the recipe home to my mom in Fairview so she could use it for one of her club meetings. I have used this recipe almost every Christmas," she wrote.

WASSAIL ✤ ✤

From Mary Jeanne Scoby Jenson

---

3 cups sugar
½ teaspoon cloves (tied in
    muslin bag if ground)
2 sticks cinnamon
1 teaspoon ginger

6 oranges, juiced
3 lemons, juiced
3 cups strong tea (1 tea bag per
    cup water)
1 quart sweet cider

Make syrup by heating 3 cups sugar and 3 cups water until sugar is dissolved. Add cloves, cinnamon and ginger and let stand overnight. Strain spices and add orange and lemon juice, tea and cider. Garnish with a slice of lemon or orange if desired.

YIELD: 18 TO 20 SERVINGS

Always Favorites, Always Modern

This mousse recipe is one of many in the first edition of *Food for Fifty* that fit the prerequisite of most home cooks today: fast and easy. You don't have to use your imagination to figure a substitute for whipping your own cream for the topping. Even easier!

Food for Five celebrated the culinary skills of a whole department in 1984. But in many cases, the busy faculty and students had the same needs: quick. This microwave snack recipe fits the bill for spur-of-the-moment celebration.

❖❖ BISQUE MOUSSE OR PEANUT BRITTLE FLUFF

Adapted from Food for Fifty *(1937)*

| 1 quart whipping cream | 1 pound peanut brittle, ground |

Whir peanut brittle in a food processor until fine. Whip cream until stiff and fold in peanut brittle. Pour into cold molds and freeze without stirring. Or serve the mixture, without freezing, on angel food cake, on pound cake or atop a hot fudge sundae.

CARMEL CORN IN BAG ✥ ✥

From Mary Frank
Published in Food for Five

½ cup butter or margarine	¼ cup corn syrup
½ teaspoon butter flavoring, if desired	1 teaspoon vinegar
	½ teaspoon baking soda
1 cup brown sugar	6 quarts popped corn

Mix butter, flavoring, sugar, syrup and vinegar in a large glass mixing bowl. Cook on high for 1½ to 2 minutes or until mixture boils. After it begin boiling, cook on high for 2 more minutes. Add soda. Put popped corn in a large unused paper bag. Pour in sauce. Close sack and shake.

Put in microwave on high for 1½ minutes. Shake and turn bag. Repeat two more times.

Spread caramel corn on waxed paper or buttered foil. Separate as it cools.

YIELD: 24 CUPS

Helen Brockman's Fashionable Touch

Orange Kiss-Me Cake was served at the funeral of Helen Brockman, a New York fashion designer turned K-State professor, who died in 2008 at age 105. It was one of her many signatures.

The original recipe won the $25,000 first prize in the 1950 Pillsbury Bake-Off Contest. Mrs. Brockman wrote, "I cut the recipe out of the newspaper and have used it a great many times. Along the way I have made extensive changes, as you would see if you were to compare my recipe with the original."

Mrs. Brockman was also famous for her Manhattan cocktails. She kept the makings in the freezer so ice wouldn't dilute the mixture.

She taught at the New York Fashion Institute of Technology before joining the K-State Department of Clothing and Textiles in 1968. She wrote *The Theory of Fashion Design*, a cookbook and two autobiographies—one abridged, one not so much.

The recipe, baked for her funeral by Wade Radina at Radina's, was printed on the back of the funeral program. I have reproduced it exactly (but fixed a couple of typos) because it is written with such charm and detail. However, nowhere does it indicate the size of the cake pan to use. I tested using a 9 x 13-inch pan and it worked perfectly. Mrs. Brockman probably would have been embarrassed by the omission.

✤✤ ORANGE KISS-ME CAKE UPDATED

From Helen Brockman

"INGREDIENTS:	
Golden Raisins [8 oz.]	1 cup Sugar
¼ cup Sugar	2 Large Eggs
¼ teaspoon Cinnamon	2 cups Flour
1 cup English Walnuts	1 teaspoon Baking Soda
1 large Navel Orange	1 teaspoon Salt
¼ lb. Butter [1 stick]	1 cup Half & Half
	⅓ cup Rum

Prepare the Raisins – Measure 1 cup of hot tap water into the 2-cup measuring cup. Add enough raisins to fill the cup, then leave them soaking in the water until time to process them.

Preparing the Topping for the Cake – Measure ¼ cup of sugar into a small soup bowl. Add ¼ teaspoon of cinnamon. Use the table fork to mix it into the sugar. Measure 1 cup of broken English Walnuts into the food processor. Chop them until the largest pieces are about the size of corn kernels. Use the rubber scraper to transfer them to the soup bowl and mix them into the sugar with the fork.

Prepare the Grated Orange Rind for the Topping – Lay the cheese grater section with the sharpest teeth on a piece of wax paper and grate the orange rind over it. Grate the orange all the way around. Add all of the gratings to the topping and stir them into it with the fork.

Prepare the Silvered Orange Sections for the Cake – Lay the orange on the cutting board and use the slicing knife to cut all of the rind off from the orange, including the white inner layer. Then remove each little orange section from its casing, in turn, and lay it on the cutting board to cut it into 10 or more thin silvers. Lay the silvers in the other soup bowl as you cut them to await their turn to be added to the batter.

Prepare the Cake–Pan Liner – Turn the cake pan upside down on a piece of wax paper to mark around it with the point of the paring knife. Cut around the paper on the mark with the shears and then cut a diagonal slash about an inch long into each corner of the paper. Then lay the paper aside.

OVEN – Turn the oven heat to 350° and set the timer for 30 minutes.

Process the Butter – Cut the butter [if frozen] into several pieces. Lay them in the cake pan and put it in the oven for 3 or 4 minutes, or just long enough to melt the butter. Wait until the butter is barely warm before using it.

Process the Sugar with the Eggs & Butter – Measure the sugar into the 12-cup mixing bowl. Break the eggs over the 4-cup bowl and let the whites fall into it. Add the yolks directly to the sugar. Use the slotted stirring spoon then mix them into it. Continue to stir the mixture until the eggs have melted the sugar enough to form a soft ball in the mixing bowl. Pour the melted butter into the bowl with one hand while you stir it in with the other hand. Use the rubber scraper to get all of the melted butter out of the baking pan.

Arrange the Wax Paper in the Baking Pan – Position the piece of wax paper that you have prepared in the bottom of the baking pan. If you arrange it evenly, it will rise about half an inch on all 4 sides. Fold the diagonal corners over and make a smooth, tight fit against the pan all the way around.

Process the Dry Ingredients – Measure the flour, soda, and salt into the strainer which you have set over the 4-cup measuring cup. Sift them into the cup which will get them properly mixed.

Process the Raisins and Half & Half – Use your hand to squeeze the water out of the raisins. Transfer them to the food processor as you work. Discard the water – about ¾ cup. Chop the raisins in the food processor until they lose their identity. Add the half & half and run the processor until the raisins absorb the half & half and the mixture thickens. Then remove the processor lid and cutting blade and set its bowl beside the mixing bowl.

Mix the Batter – Use 2 tablespoons to add the flour mixture and the raisin mixture to the sugar mixture in the big mixing bowl. First add a heaping tablespoon of flour and stir until the batter is smooth, then add a heaping tablespoon of the raisin mix and stir until its combined. Continue these alternate additions until all the flour and the raisin mix have been assimilated.

Add the Orange Silvers – Use the stirring spoon to pick the orange silvers out of their juice in the soup bowl and to stir them gently into the batter.

The Final Step – Beat the egg whites stiff enough to match the consistency of the batter. Use the rubber scraper to transfer them to it. Then fold them in until they are combined and totally "lost". Use the rubber scraper to transfer the batter to the cake pan, spreading it evenly into the corners.

Bake the Cake – The timer should have rung by the time the cake is in the pan. Set it in the middle of the lower oven shelf. Set the timer for 50 minutes. Begin to test the cake with a toothpick as soon as you smell it, which may be 45 minutes. It is done when the toothpick comes out of the middle of the cake clean.

Out of the Oven – Set the cake on the cooling rack while you run the paring knife around the edge of the pan to make sure the cake is not stuck to it at any point. Then move the cake off the cooling rack, turn the rack over on it, and then invert cake pan and rack together. Lift the pan off the cake and immediately begin to loosen one side of the wax paper with the paring knife so that you can pull it back over the cake, and off. Act promptly or this feat becomes difficult. Put the cake pan back over the cake while it cools on the cooling rack for an hour, then return it to the cake pan, on the cooling rack.

Add the Topping and the Rum – While the cake is still warm, spread the sugar/walnut topping evenly over its surface with the rubber scraper. Then drizzle the rum over the cake. A good way to get the rum lightly and evenly distributed is to use a small salt shaker.

Serve and/or Store the Cake – As soon as you have drizzled the rum, cover the cake with plastic wrap to permit it to cool in a leisurely way so that the rum can really penetrate it. Wait at least 6 hours – or until tomorrow – before serving it. It will keep nicely at room temperature for 3 or 4 days. After that I cut the remainder into serving slices, wrap them in a plastic wrap and freeze them. Then I warm them in the microwave just before serving."

Celebrating with Science

Kris Hennessy, who has doctor of veterinary medicine and PhD degrees from K-State, leads Hennessy Research Associates in Kansas City. Her company researches and develops animal health products, vaccines and diagnostic tests. She does not perform tests, she develops them. Some of her most successful work has been with horses.

Her fascination with chemistry, research and development lead to a curious second business: Dark Horse Distillery. Hennessy founded the company in 2010 and calls it "a bit of maverick, a splash of daring and a commitment to hand-crafted spirits made from local grains."

One of the products is small batch Reunion Rye Whiskey. Rye has been called the Comeback Kid, a key spirit trend in 2013. To celebrate, may we suggest it as an alternative to a Sazerac?

KANSAS RYE WHISKEY CHOCOLATE MALT ✤ ✤

1 quart rich vanilla ice cream
¼ cup whipping cream
½ cup cocoa powder

1 tablespoon plus 1 teaspoon
   malt powder
½ cup rye whiskey
Freshly grated nutmeg

Combine all ingredients in jar of high-speed blender. Blend until smooth and creamy. Pour into glasses and garnish with a little nutmeg grated over the top.

YIELD: 4 SERVINGS

To be continued...

THE STORY OF K-STATE'S CONTRIBUTION to the cuisine and nutrition of the world will not end after its first 150 years, of course.

Words such as sustainability, food safety, food security and functional foods have infiltrated our vocabulary. How will the world feed a population that is expected to exceed 9 billion people by 2050? Will our food be safe? How will our food choices impact health? How can we make better choices?

A portion of the answers will come from K-State:

Bikram Gill, professor of plant pathology, works with an international team of researchers on wheat genetics. "Wheat has the largest genome among crop plants and this is the biggest map as yet assembled for any organism, animal or plant," he explains. This research will help scientists battle disease resistance and other production issues.

Professors Edgar Chambers IV, Delores Chambers and **the Sensory Analysis Center team** continue to help elucidate consumer eating behavior through their teaching and research. They study properties of food products; conduct research on actual and recommended portion sizes; and study the ways in which people shop, store, prepare and eat food. All of this leads to a better understanding of the types of food options consumers will accept and why.

Jim Drouillard, professor of animal sciences and industry, is developing a technique that enriches ground beef with omega-3 fatty acids—fatty acids that have been shown to reduce heart disease, cholesterol and high blood pressure.

Associate Professor Mark Haub, human nutrition, studies the link between foods and diabetes, obesity and gut health.

Charles W. Rice, professor of soil microbiology, continues his work on soil microbiology and climate change that affect the grassland and fields that grow our food.

Elizabeth Boyle, professor in animal sciences and industry, works to enhance the quality and safety of meat products.

Ted Schroeder, professor of agricultural economics, points out, "Technology discovery, technology development and technology adoption are huge in terms of food prices, who will produce the food and how we're going to feed the world."

After 150 years, the story of food and K–State remains the story of understanding nature, of harnessing science and of making friends, conversation and memories over a good plate of steak and pie.

So the Wildcat band plays on. The professors keep teaching. The researchers continue making discoveries. K–State stays ever serious about its mission of education, research and extension. It continues to impact what people around the world put on their tables and tailgates.

BUT WHERE ARE THE CINNAMON ROLLS?

Teatime to Tailgates is far from comprehensive. I left out persimmons and California date ranchers who got their start at K-State. Extensive work with potatoes and watermelon is missing, too. A whole book could be devoted to picnics, banquets and the dining establishments past and present that didn't make it into this one. A yawning hole is the lack of a cinnamon roll recipe. Cinnamon rolls deserve an entire chapter. Maybe a book. Our bows to the ubiquitous Kansas sweet rolls—a student once asked me why people in Kansas always served cinnamon rolls with chili—are the K-State Crown (p. 165) and Cohen's Chicken House Orange Rolls (p. 122).

Not included are many who influence what we put on our plates—those who feed us from their kitchens in eating establishments in Manhattan and all over the country; those who teach others to make good food choices and to plan and manage food operations; those who invent, grow and process our victuals.

We salute them nonetheless.

Selected Bibliography

"A look at the early years of Manhattan's women's clubs." *Manhattan Mercury* [Manhattan, KS] 5 Sept. 2003.

Averill, Thomas Fox. "Kansas Wheat Harvest." *Kansas History: A Journal of the Central Plains.* 23.1-2 (2000): 112–119.

Bamberg, Elma L. " 'Give Us This Day Our Daily Bread': A Harvest Memoir." *Kansas History: A Journal of the Central Plains.* 23.1-2 (2000): 6–11.

Beecher, Catherine Esther and Harriet Beecher Stowe. *The American Woman's Home: Or, Principles of Domestic Science.* New York: J. B. Ford and Company, 1869.

Bidwell, Orville and William E. Roth. "The Land and the Soil." *The Rise of the Wheat State: A History of Kansas Agriculture, 1861-1986.* Eds. George E. Ham and Robin Higham. Manhattan, KS: Sunflower University Press, 1987.

Bieberly, Frank G. "Other Crops in the Wheat State." *The Rise of the Wheat State: A History of Kansas Agriculture, 1861-1986.* Eds. George E. Ham and Robin Higham. Manhattan, KS: Sunflower University Press, 1987.

Carey, James C. *Kansas State University: The Quest for Identity.* Lawrence: Regents Press of Kansas, 1977.

Colt, Miriam Davis. *Went to Kansas.* 1886. Worcester, MA: Readex Microprint Corp., 1966.

Cordier, Mary Hurlbut. *Schoolwomen of the Prairies and Plains.* Albuquerque: The University of New Mexico Press, 1992.

Dary, David. *More True Tales of Old Time Kansas.* Lawrence, KS: University Press of Kansas, 1987.

Davis, Kenneth S. *Kansas, a Bicentennial History.* New York: Norton, 1976.

Department of Dietetics, Restaurant and Institutional Management. *Food for Five*. Manhattan, KS: Kansas State University, 1984.

Deyo, Charles W. "Flour Milling in Kansas State University." *The Rise of the Wheat State: A History of Kansas Agriculture, 1861-1986*. Eds. George E. Ham and Robin Higham. Manhattan, KS: Sunflower University Press, 1987.

"Editors' Table: Ladies in Agricultural Colleges." *Godey's Lady's Book and Magazine*, Feb. 1870.

Fairbanks, Gustave E. "Mechanizing the Kansas Farm." *The Rise of the Wheat State: A History of Kansas Agriculture, 1861-1986*. Eds. George E. Ham and Robin Higham. Manhattan, KS: Sunflower University Press, 1987.

Feast of Nations Committee. *World Cookbook*. Manhattan, KS: Kansas State University International Coordinating Council, 1973.

"Fifty Years of Home Economics Education at K.S.A.C." *Home Economics News* 1.2 (April 1925).

Good, Don L. "The Beef Cattle Industry." *The Rise of the Wheat State: A History of Kansas Agriculture, 1861-1986*. Eds. George E. Ham and Robin Higham. Manhattan, KS: Sunflower University Press, 1987.

Graber, Kay. *Nebraska Pioneer Cookbook*. Lincoln: University of Nebraska Press, 1974.

Gregory, Annie R. *Woman's Home Receipt Book*. Chicago: W.S. Reeve Publishing Co., 1902.

Gumprecht, Blake. *The American College Town*. Amherst, MA: University of Massachusetts Press, 2008.

Gunn, Virginia Railsback. *Educating Strong Womanly Women: Kansas Shapes the Western Home Economics Movement, 1860-1914*. Diss. University of Akron, 1992.

Gunn, Virginia Railsback. "Industrialists Not Butterflies: Women's Higher Education at Kansas State Agricultural College, 1873-1882." *Kansas History* 18.1 (1995): 2–17.

Ham, George E. "An Agronomist's View." *The Rise of the Wheat State: A History of Kansas Agriculture, 1861-1986*. Eds. George E. Ham and Robin Higham. Manhattan, KS: Sunflower University Press, 1987.

Ham, George E., and Robin Higham, eds. *The Rise of the Wheat State: A History of Kansas Agriculture, 1861-1986*. Manhattan, KS: Sunflower University Press, 1987.

Harner, Ivy Frances. *A Pioneer Girl: An Autobiography*. Sedona, AZ: Harner Selvidge, 1944.

Harper, Josephine. "History of the Domestic Science Club of Manhattan." Read at the club's 45th birthday, May 55, 1921.

Harvey, Fred. *Hospitality Cookbook: Famous Recipes that Were Served Along the Santa Fe Railroad Route from Kansas to California*. Grand Canyon, AZ: Fred Harvey Co, c. 1980.

Hayter, Barbara Bonzer. "Mean cuisines and cool hotels." *K-Stater*, Fall 2005: 19–25.

Henderson, James David. *Meals by Fred Harvey: A Phenomenon of the American West*. Fort Worth, TX: Texas Christian University Press, 1969.

Heyne. E. G. "The Development of Wheat in Kansas." *The Rise of the Wheat State: A History of Kansas Agriculture, 1861-1986*. Eds. George E. Ham and Robin Higham. Manhattan, KS: Sunflower University Press, 1987.

Higham, Robin. "A Historian's View." *The Rise of the Wheat State: A History of Kansas Agriculture, 1861-1986*. Eds. George E. Ham and Robin Higham. Manhattan, KS: Sunflower University Press, 1987.

Hoeflin, Ruth. *History of a College: From Woman's Course to Home Economics to Human Ecology, 1873-1988 Kansas State University*. Manhattan, KS: College of Human Ecology, Kansas State University, 1988.

Holme, Kenneth L., ed. *Covered Wagon Women: Diaries and Letters from the Western Trail 1840-1890*. Spokane, WA: The Author H. Clark Co., 1993.

Isern, Thomas D. "Wheat Explorer the World Over: Mark Carleton of Kansas." *Kansas History: A Journal of the Central Plains.* 23.1-2 (2000): 12–25.

Jones, Carolyn. *The First One Hundred Years: A History of the City of Manhattan, Kansas 1855-1955.* Manhattan: Manhattan Centennial, Inc., 1955.

Jones, Nellie Sawyer Kedzie. "Pioneering in Home Economics." *K-Stater.* Manhattan, KS: K-State Alumni Association, October 1954.

Jordan, Carole. "The Kansas State Board of Agriculture." *The Rise of the Wheat State: A History of Kansas Agriculture, 1861-1986.* Eds. George E. Ham and Robin Higham. Manhattan, KS: Sunflower University Press, 1987.

Kansas 4-H Foundation. *Essence of Kansas: 4-H Cookbook, Taste Two.* Nashville: Favorite Recipes Press, 1994.

Kansas 4-H Foundation. *Essence of Kansas! Taste--: Food Experiences with 4-H Friends.* Nashville: Favorite Recipes Press, 1988.

Kansas 4-H Foundation. *Essence of Kansas: Taste Three*, Centennial 4-H Cookbook. Manhattan, KS: Kansas 4-H Foundation, 2000.

Kansas Gold: Historical Notes and Heritage Recipes from the First Fifty Years of the Kansas Wheat Commission. Manhattan, KS: Kansas Wheat Commission, 2007.

Kansas State Agricultural College. *Kansas Kook-Book for Kansas Kooks: For the Use of Housewives.* Topeka: Kansas Farmer Press, 1900.

Kellett, Carol. *History of the College of Human Ecology.* Work in progress.

Kelly, Kathleen. *Favorite Recipes: 35 years of Kansas Prizewinners from the Wichita Eagle.* Wichita, KS: Wichita Eagle and Beacon Pub. Co., 1993.

Kennedy, Nancy. *The Ford Treasury of Favorite Recipes from Famous Eating Places.* 3 v. New York: Simon and Schuster, 1950–59.

Kids in the Kitchen: A Cookbook for Young People. Manhattan, KS: KSU Child Care Cooperative, 1987.

Koch, Berl A. "Other Livestock Industries." *The Rise of the Wheat State: A History of Kansas Agriculture, 1861-1986.* Eds. George E. Ham and Robin Higham. Manhattan, KS: Sunflower University Press, 1987.

Koelliker, James K. "Water." *The Rise of the Wheat State: A History of Kansas Agriculture, 1861-1986.* Eds. George E. Ham and Robin Higham. Manhattan, KS: Sunflower University Press, 1987.

K-State Student Alumni Board. *Cats in the Kitchen.* Kearney, NE: Morris Press Cookbooks, 2009.

KSU Dames Favorite Recipes. Manhattan, KS: Kansas State University, 1975.

K-Taste! K-State Housing & Dining Services Recipe Collection. Manhattan, KS: Kansas State University, 2006.

Luchetti, Cathy. *Women of the West.* St. George, UT: Antelope Island Press, 1982.

Lynn-Sherow, Bonnie. "Beyond Winter Wheat: The USDA Extension Service and Kansas Wheat Production in the Twentieth Century." *Kansas History: A Journal of the Central Plains.* 23.1–2 (2000): 100–111.

MacKenzie, Colin. *Mackenzie's Five Thousand Receipts in all the Useful and Domestic Arts: Constituting a Complete Practical Library.* Philadelphia: T. Ellwood Zell, 1854.

Malin, James C. *Winter Wheat in the Golden Belt of Kansas: A Study I Adaption to Subhumid Geographical Environment.* New York: Octagon Books, 1973.

McCaffree, Mary Ellen and Anne McNamee Corbett. *Politics of the Possible, The Decade our American Democracy Worked.* McCaffree Publishing, 2011.

Miner, H. Craig. Kansas: *The History of the Sunflower State, 1854-2000.* Lawrence: University Press of Kansas, 2002.

Muilenburg, Grace, Floyd W. Smith, and Lowell Brandner. "From Desert to Breadbasket: Developing Kansas's Land Resources." Manhattan: Agricultural Experiment Station, Kansas State University, 1976.

Niles-Beattie, Anita. *Pioneers of the Flint Hills: From Earliest Times to 1900*. Hillsboro: Hearth Publishing, 1996.

Nugent, Walter. *Into the West: The Story of Its People*. New York, Knopf, 1999.

Oleen, Jean. *Bell Ringing Recipes: Chapter H of PEO Sisterhood, Council Grove, KS*. Lenexa, KS: Cookbook Publishers, 1979.

Oliver, Sandy. *Food History News*. Web. http://www.foodhistorynews.com

Olson, Kevin G. W. *Frontier Manhattan: Yankee Settlement to Kansas Town, 1854-1894*. Lawrence: University Press of Kansas, 2012.

Olver, Lynne. *The Food Timeline*. Web. http://www.foodtimeline.org

Paddleford, Clementine. *A Flower for My Mother*. New York: Holt, 1958.

Paddleford, Clementine. *Cooking Young Cookbook*. New York: Pocket Books, 1966.

Paddleford, Clementine. *How America Eats*. New York: Charles Scribner's Sons, 1960.

Paulsen, Gary M. *Keeping up with Research 136: A History of Wheat Improvement at Kansas State University*. Kansas State University Agriculture Experiment Station and Cooperative Extension Service, March 2003. Web. http://www.ksre.ksu.edu/historicpublications/Pubs/SRL136.pdf

Paulsen, Gary M. *Some Contributions of K-State Agronomists To World Agriculture During the 20th Century*. K-State Research and Extension, Nov. 2001. Web. http://www.ksre.ksu.edu/historicpublications/Pubs/AGRON.pdf

Poling-Kempes, Lesley. *The Harvey Girls: Women Who Opened the West*. New York: Marlowe & Company, 1989.

Prawl, Nancy. "A Century of Traditions: 100 Years of Kansas State University Social Club." Kansas State University Social Club Centennial Luncheon. Manhattan Country Club, Manhattan, KS. 1 Nov. 2011. Lecture.

Ramos, Mary G. "Cattle Drives Started in Earnest After the Civil War." *Texas Almanac 1990-1991*. Ed. Mike Kingston. Denton, TX: Texas State Historical Association, 1989.

Reber, Patricia Bixler. *Culinary History Online*. Web. http://www.hearthcook.com

Riney-Kehrberg, Pamela. "Women in Wheat Country." *Kansas History: A Journal of the Central Plains*. 23.1-2 (2000): 56–71.

Root, Waverly, and Richard de Rochemont. *Eating in America*. New York: William Morrow, 1976.

Saul, Norman E. "Mill Town Kansas in the Age of Turkey Red." *Kansas History: A Journal of the Central Plains*. 23.1-2 (2000): 26–41.

Schoeff, Robert W. "The Grain Elevator." *The Rise of the Wheat State: A History of Kansas Agriculture, 1861-1986*. Eds. George E. Ham and Robin Higham. Manhattan, KS: Sunflower University Press, 1987.

"Semi-centennial Anniversary Edition." *Manhattan Nationalist* [Manhattan, KS] 16 June 1910.

Sjo, John. "The Family Farm Becomes a Business Enterprise: 1860-1980." *The Rise of the Wheat State: A History of Kansas Agriculture, 1861-1986*. Eds. George E. Ham and Robin Higham. Manhattan, KS: Sunflower University Press, 1987.

Slagg, Winifred N. *Riley County Kansas: A Story of Early Settlements, Rich Valleys, Azure Skies and Sunflowers*. Manhattan: Winifred N. Slagg, 1968.

Socolofsky, Homer E. "The Agricultural Heritage." *The Rise of the Wheat State: A History of Kansas Agriculture, 1861-1986*. Eds. George E. Ham and Robin Higham. Manhattan, KS: Sunflower University Press, 1987.

Socolofsky, Homer E. "The Culture of Wheat in Kansas." *Kansas History: A Journal of the Central Plains*. 23.1-2 (2000): 2–5.

Sorenson, L. Orlo. "Transportation Development and Kansas Agriculture." *The Rise of the Wheat State: A History of Kansas Agriculture, 1861-1986*. Eds. George E. Ham and Robin Higham. Manhattan, KS: Sunflower University Press, 1987.

Teagarden, E. H., R. L. Johnson and R. O. Graham. *The Kansas Cooperative Extension Service: Extending the University to the People, 1914-1989*. K-State Research and Extension, 1991. Web. http://www.ksre.ksu.edu/ historicpublications/Extension_History.htm

Vollmar, Karla and Grace Lang. *Cookie Classics*. Manhattan, KS: Cooperative Extension Service, 1980.

Walters, Dan. *Aggieville 1889-1989: 100 Years of the Aggieville Tradition*. Manhattan: Varney's Bookstore, 1989.

Walters, John D. *History of the Kansas State Agricultural College*. Manhattan: Kansas State Agricultural College, 1909.

Westbrook, Virginia M. Introduction. *Buckeye Cookery and Practical Housekeeping*. Ed. Estelle Woods Wilcox. 1880. St. Paul: Minnesota Historical Society Press, 1988.

Whipple, Leslie J. *The Oregon Trail Cookbook*. Bend, OR: Maverick Publications, 1992.

Whitehead, Jessup. *The Chicago Herald Cooking School: A Professional Cook's Book for Household Use*. Chicago: Daily National Hotel Reporter, 1883.

Willard, Julius T. *History of the Kansas State College of Agriculture and Applied Science*. Manhattan: KSC Press, 1940.

Williams, Jacqueline. *Wagon Wheel Kitchens*. Lawrence: University Press of Kansas, 1993.

Zabicka, Dorata. *International Cookbook: 44 Recipes from Around the World*. Manhattan, KS: Kansas State University International Coordinating Council, 1994.

Index

About the Author

JANE P. MARSHALL grew up on a farm in the Kansas Flint Hills where she plowed and baled hay before tractors had computers and air conditioners.

She used to claim she was probably the only newspaper features editor in the country who could take a chicken from the coop to the table. However, she preferred not to. After more than 25 years as a newspaper editor and reporter, Marshall took a fork in the road. She moved back to her home state and teaches food writing and food history at Kansas State University. She also is communications coordinator for the College of Human Ecology.

Marshall has a home economics/journalism degree from K-State and a master's degree from the University of St. Thomas in Houston. She is a founding member and first president of Journalism and Women Symposium, past president of the American Association of Sunday and Features Editors, and author of one children's book. She served as features editor in Fort Worth, Denver, and Houston where she also was food editor.

PHOTOGRAPHY BY JOHN W. THURSTON; 1952 CHEVROLET PICKUP RESTORED AND OWNED BY BRUCE SNEAD; VEGETABLES BY KANSAS FARMERS.